I0421156

TABLE OF CONTENTS

Lending and Venture Funds for Developing Countries

Access to Funds and Mobile Banking

Identifying the Beneficiary without disclosure in society

Developing their Mind Map

Identify their Interest and Develop Custom Solutions

Put them into training and prepare them for Work force

Train them Creating Micro Entrepreneurs

Assign a Mentor – Sometimes Pat on The Back Does the Job!

Develop Call Center Approach for ROI Evaluation of your beneficiaries

Online Counselling and MIS systems

Three M's - Monitor, Mentor and Motivate until they reach their Finishing Line

Bring them back as Alumni and increase your Out reach

Compliments - Sleep well! Good wishes

SOCIAL ENTREPRENEURSHIP as a REMEDY TO POVERTY

Peer Lending, Micro finance and Mobile banking all were good till 2015.

Now is the Age for what we call **SOCIAL ENTREPRENEURS**

A complete guide book for **Not for Profits and Social Development Professionals**

ABOUT FARID PREMANI - AUTHOR

Farid Premani is a technologist and social entrepreneur with extensive experience in public speaking and development projects. He has worked in more than eight different countries from belt of Asia to Europe and US

Having developed and assisted humongous businesses from scratch both in corporate and micro sectors he carries passion to serve community and build those who we call **UNDERSERVED** – CREATING ENTREPRENEURS.
Poverty is not only lack of resources but also **ABSENCE OF VISSION**. Hence it's our responsibility to help others AS AND WHEN WE CAN being called amongst **BLESSED**!

1. Introduction

How many of you enjoy a safe and secure life, with a stable employment and money to take care of your everyday needs? I know that most of you who read this book fit this category; however while we are fortunate enough to fend for ourselves, there is a large part of the world reveling in poverty where people find it difficult to not only make ends meet, but also to have a proper meal a day.

Yes, while we enjoy the luxury of fast food, multiplexes, advanced technology and cozy homes, many people in countries like Africa and some parts of Asia like India and Bangladesh, people lie hungry without any shelter.

This is all because of poverty, which is mainly a mindset. It's nothing permanent. It's just that the people living in poverty do not know how they can come out of their misery. If they do, they don't have the necessary assistance and funds to live a normal life.

It is thus left to us, those who have a home to return to every night and a hot meal three times a day to do something about this. We need to show them that their poverty is nothing permanent and that they are not destined to die in poverty. we have to show them how it's possible to earn a living doing things they are good at and even run businesses and thus provide employment to others in their tribe.

They do not have the means or the ideas to do all this; it is left to us in the developed countries to do something about this. We have to assist them and show them all about entrepreneurship, how it can help create jobs for people, how entrepreneurship can convert a small business into a thriving business competing with other businesses and how they too can live a normal life like all of us.

It is while keeping all this in mind that this book was written, to show how we can make an influence on the less fortunate. How we can show them that they are not actually 'less fortunate', but are just ignorant to the many opportunities available today. While it may not have been so easy to eradicate poverty before, today technology has made it a much easier task.

So this is what this book is about, how it is possible to eradicate poverty. How the mobile phone can help do this. How and why mentors help in eradicating poverty. How and why a mind map is necessary. And the importance of workforce alumni.

All it takes is some time reading this book and you are sure to get inspired with some ideas and means of helping the less fortunate and thus giving you a sense of satisfaction for doing something great for the less fortunate by providing them with an idea, a means and some assistance at coming out of their misery.

2. Poverty – A Mindset & Lack of Resources

Poverty. It prevails all over the world, and something has to be done about this. This book is an attempt to not actually end it, or predict what its future consequences are. It is sort of an explanation of what can happen if nothing is done to eradicate it and how it is actually possible for people around the world to help each other come out of poverty.

If you look around, you will find that today about 8 million people across the world die of poverty, only because they are so poor they cannot stay alive. If we put some efforts, our generation can indeed put an end to it by the year 2025.

Moreover, the cause of all this death is poverty. People not being able to access the right medical treatment, not living in sanitary or hygienic conditions, poor nutrition and ignorance are all a consequence of being extremely poor.

The newspapers give you news about thousands of children dying of malaria, mothers and fathers dying from tuberculosis, thousands of young adults dying of aids and even more dying from other health conditions like diarrhea, respiratory infection and all other diseases which people weakened from chronic hunger suffer from.

Even if some of them do manage to reach hospitals, they only end up dying there because of a lack of medication. Others die just because they can't afford to buy something as cheap as antimalarial bed nets and safe drinking water.

The saddest thing is the world does not know about all this. The only thing the world knows is figures; however they don't know how much of daily struggles all these people go through only because of their poverty.

Yes, it's true that since the drastic event 9/11, the US has launched a massive attack at eradicating terror worldwide. However in the process, they have failed at tackling the main causes of global insanity. So no matter how many billings the US spends on terror, they will never actually be able to buy peace in the world if they don't spend a meagre amount of this, say a thirtieth of it, to help the world's poorest of the poor. It is these masses of people who have become so destabilized in life because of their poverty and this has in turn lead to a growing number of havens of violence, unrest and even terrorism amidst these masses.

The irony of everything is that all US has to spend to help at eradicating it is about 15 cents for every $100 of the US gross national product or GNP. Moreover, this share has continually been dropping over the decades and has ended up to become only a fraction of what the US has promised, but failed to give.

The amount is even much less than what the US should devote to solve the problem of extreme poverty and in the process, provide for US national security. And this book is just an attempt to help make the right choices to end poverty, and in the process, lead to a much safer world where there is more reference and respect for the human life.

I have over the years visited and worked in over a hundred countries constituting of more than 90% of the world's population. These visits have helped me see the world through vantage points and realize our planet's actual position- the causes for the rampant poverty in so many countries, the effects of rich-country policies and future possibilities.

With this knowledge, I have managed to observe and even contribute a bit to some real successful changes in the world economy like the end of hyperinflations, the implementation of new and stable national currencies, cancelling of unpayable debts, starting the Global Fund to fight diseases like Malaria, AIDS and TB and the implementation of modern drug treatment to use in the impoverished HIV infected very poor people.

Through my observations, I also learnt that what the rich world claims to do to help the poor is not always true. I also learnt that if properly channeled and implemented, it is however possible to use the massive power found in our generation's hand and put an end to the horrendous suffering the extremely poor go through.

While some parts of the world are spiraling upwards in a whirlwind of progress and unprecedented prosperity, there are other parts of the world which is spiraling downwards in hunger, diseases and impoverishment.

Instead of giving a lecture to the underprivileged of their not doing enough with their lives, its better and more helpful to them if you help them climb the ladder of development. Teach or rather guide them up, or at least let them gain a foothold on the bottom rung, so that they can then slowly but surely climb up the ladder alone, without your help.

Teach them that poverty is a mindset, and how it's possible to come out of their dire situation by working and earning money instead of just waiting for someone to donate money to them. They are not aware of the many opportunities available to earn money and grow stable in life. By teaching them about these options, and helping them work and earn something, they can slowly come out of their poverty plight.

This is something which cannot be reached by a single person, overnight. This has to be a combined effort by everyone all over the world, for you and me. We have to work together to help the poorest of the poor. Help them to fight disease by educating them and providing the right and necessary infrastructure.

Once the underprivileged grow privileged enough to experience and relish basic infrastructure like roads, ports and power in their towns and villages, they experience a renewed hope and light in the future. They feel there actually is a chance of their coming out of their predicament, and for their country to develop.

An improved infrastructure along with an improved health capital of improved health and education, opens up the doors of development and progress in any locality. In fact, it is the absence of these preconditions which lead to markets bypassing a large part of the world and not being able to tap the resources in these parts of the world, which in turn leaves all the inhabitants here impoverished and suffering in their lives without any respite.

It is only through a collective and collaborative action implemented through the government's provision of proper health, education, infrastructure and even foreign assistance is it possible for the underprivileged to be a part of, and experience economic success.

It was about 85 years ago that the great British economist John Maynard Keynes started worrying and thinking about the dire consequences of the Great Depression. It was the huge despair and unhappiness around him that instigated him to write the Economic Possibilities for our Grandchildren in the year 1930.

After looking at all the suffering and duress surrounding him, he predicted that all the poverty which prevailed in Great Britain and other industrial countries would finally come to an end in his grandchildren's day. He had predicted that this would be somewhere towards the end of the twentieth century.

He emphasized on a need of using the help of both science and technology, and all the advances in technology to help underpin the economic growth at a compounded interest so that there is sufficient economic growth to put an end to the age-old economic problems people face of having enough food to eat and enough income to help meet the other basic needs of life. Looking at today's rich countries, where there no longer is any extreme poverty, and that most of the cases of extreme poverty is disappearing in most of today's middle-income countries, it proves that Keynes may have just got it all right all those years back.

This is why I suggest, and believe that if we too invoke and use the same logic, we can safely declare that it's possible to eradicate the extreme poverty which exists in today's society in our times, and not wait till our grandchildren's time.

It is the combination of the wealth generated from the rich world, the power which is and can be generated through today's vast storehouses of knowledge and the slowly but surely reducing number of people in the world that no longer needs help to escape from poverty all show that it is indeed possible to put an end to all the reigning poverty within the year 2025.

Keynes had also wondered how exactly his grandchildren and their society will be able to manage and use all the wealth they accumulate, and the freedom they finally attain from their age-old struggle for daily survival.

We too should think, and ponder on this very question. We should wonder if we will ever have the capacity and proper judgment to wisely use all our accumulated wealth, if we will be able to finally heal our divided planet, if we will actually be able to put an end to all the suffering those still trapped in poverty have to go through, and if it's actually possible to finally and actually forge a common bond of security, humanity and shared purpose across the multitude of cultures and regions. At the same time, we should guide them and show them that there is a light at the end of the tunnel, and that anything is possible with hard work.

Of course, don't think that this book will provide an answer to all these questions. Instead, this book is meant only to show you the way towards attaining peace and prosperity in life mainly by understanding how today's world economy has reached where it is today, and how it's possible for our next generations to mobilize all their capacities in the future twenty years so that they finally get to eliminate the extreme poverty existing all around.

It is my wish and aim that by showing all the contours of the chosen or promised path, the chances of us choosing and adapting this aim in life is increased. I am forever grateful for being able and having a chance to share whatever I felt about the world and to have an opportunity to change the economic possibilities of our time.

3. Global Picture of Poverty & Its Stages

It's easier to understand the poverty situation if you took a look at its global picture, and found out how the underprivileged actually lived. There are actually many definitions and intense debates going on about the exact number of poor people in the world, where they live and how their economic conditions and numbers seem to change with time.

For discussion purpose, it's better to distinguish the different types of poverty as extreme or absolute, moderate or relative poverty. Those living in the extreme are households which do not have the means to meet their basic needs for survival.

These are the people who don't have enough food for themselves and are thus chronically hungry, have no means to access the necessary health care, don't have the basic infrastructure of even safe drinking water and sanitation and do not have the money or means to even afford to educate some or all of their children.

Some even lack rudimentary shelter of a roof to keep the rain out of the hut, and a chimney to remove the smoke from the cook stove. They also don't have basic articles and necessary clothing like shoes. Extreme poverty usually exists only in developing countries.

In case of moderate poverty, it indicates the condition of life of people whose basic needs are only barely met. This means they have enough just to fend themselves but nothing more. The group of people who fall in the relative poverty group are a group of people whose household income level is below a fixed ratio of the average national income.

Then there are the relatively poor people who live in high-income countries who have enough to survive and live, but cannot afford cultural goods, entertainment, recreation and even quality health care and education so that they can fit into upward social mobility.

Comparative analysis

The World Bank has developed a system to carry out a comparative analysis of poverty throughout the world. They use a statistical standard where an income of $2 per day per person, which is measured based on purchasing power parity, to determine the number of extremely poor worldwide.

In another World Bank category are those who have an income of between $3 and $4 and who are considered to be moderately poor. According to their statistics, the number of extremely poor has dropped from 1.5 billion in 1981 to 1.1 billion people in 2001.

Moreover, most of the world's extremely poor, about 93% in 2001 live in East Asia, South Asia and sub-Saharan Asia. In fact, there was a substantial reduction in China and some south Asian countries mainly because of the country's rapid economic development.

However the reduction was not so marked in countries like Sri Lanka, Pakistan and Bangladesh. The number of extremely poor in East Asia has dropped from 58% in 1981 to 15% in 2001. Progress is also significantly marked in South Asia where the drop is slightly less dramatic from 52% to 31%.

It's around 10% in Latin America and relatively stuck there while the level's risen from a negligible level in 1981 to about 4% in 2001, all the consequence of communist collapse and economic transition to a market economy.

However while the number has dropped in East Asia and South Asia, it has risen in sub-Saharan Asia. Poverty has increased from 41% in 1981 to 48% in 2001 in Sub Saharan Africa while there has been no changes in Latin America. Ironically, poverty which was non-existent for some time, has resurfaced in some countries like Russia and a few former communist countries.

In case of the moderate poor who live on between $3 and $4 a day, 87% of the world's 1.6 billion are moderately poor with South Asia, East Asia and sub-Saharan Africa dominating the picture.

However the number of moderately poor in East Asia and South Asia has increased as the number of poorest households here have managed to improve their living circumstances to become moderately poor from being extremely poor. 15% of Latin Americans have however consistently lived in moderate poverty since 1981.

Collected statistics also shows that most of the countries in Sub-Saharan Africa and South Asia live in extreme poverty. However East Asia and Latin America has many countries living in moderate poverty and many which have risen beyond in recent decades.

However the precision of all this data collected by the World Bank has been questioned in debates as the World Bank had collected all this through household surveys while others have collected their data through national income accounts which shows there is faster progress in reducing poverty in Asia.

This however should not detain us as the data gives a picture true in either case, which is that extreme poverty exists in East Asia, South Asia and sub-Saharan Africa. The only thing is that the number is rising in absolute numbers in Africa but is falling in absolute numbers in the Asian regions.

Where the money goes

It was found out that a majority of the people in developing countries who lived under $2 a day spent most of the money earned on food. They spent about 55 to 80% of their income on food but lacked and had no access to basic infrastructure and owned only a few productive assets.

These people generally owned some productive assets like a bicycle, sewing machine, tractor or phone and in some cases, large proportion of poor households also owned small plots of land.

Though poor, they do at times spend on things other than food and this ownership of non-productive assets varied across countries between the rural and urban areas. For example while no one who lived with less than $2 a day owned a television in Tanzania, 57% of the people living in the same income in Hyderabad, India owned a television.

However the rates for owning a radio was higher than that of a television. More than 70% of the people living on under $2 in Peru, South Africa and Nicaragua owned radios while the ownership rates were more than 40% in other places.

Similarly, the access to electricity, water and sanitation varies widely amidst countries and regions. For example, electricity access is practically universal in Mexico and Indonesia but an in-house water and a toilet or latrine in the house is not so prevalent in Indonesia. Things are different in Tanzania where practically all poor households owned a toilet and only a few had access to in-house water or electricity.

Less satisfaction with life

Based on a poll conducted on 132 countries, on an average, it's disclosed that the people living in poor countries are less satisfied with their lives when compared to those in rich countries. If the two are compared on a scale of 1 – 10, the people of low-income countries have an average satisfaction rate of 4.3 while those in G8 countries have an average satisfaction rate of 6.7.

This is a rather large satisfaction gap between the two. The people living in Sub-Saharan Africa are once again exceptionally dissatisfied as more than half of them live under $2.25 a day and some more just above the line. More than 2.5 billion people or rather three-quarters of the population in Sub-Saharan Africa live on less than $2 a day.

This shows that the people in Sub-Saharan Africa are definitely worse off, which indicates that the chances of them dying prematurely is much higher than those living in the wealthier parts of the year.

On the contrary, if they manage to live past the age of 5, then there is a strong chance of their living to the age of 60 or so. This proves that if it is possible to save a life from just one cause of death like a disease or malnutrition, it is possible to save a person who can live quite longer.

The hardest problem people in Sub-Saharan Africa and other extremely poor countries in economic development is getting onto the first rung of the ladder to economic development. All those households and countries here at the bottom of the world's income distribution are in other words stuck here.

There are however countries like India and Bangladesh which are already making some progress here, even though the progress may be a bit slow and uneven. It is our duty and part of our generations' challenge to help these people, the poorest of the poor, come out of their miserable life by showing them work opportunities and means of earning a living so that they too can climb up the ladder of economic development. This leads to an end of poverty, which not only spells the end of extreme suffering, but also the start of economic progress and its accompanying economic development.

So when I talk of the 'end of poverty' here, I refer to two closely connected and related objectives. The first objective is to put an end to all the misery and horrible plight a sixth of humanity lives in, in continual struggle for survival.

I, and everyone should feel and agree that everybody on earth should be able to enjoy the basic standards of life which includes nutrition, water, sanitation, health, shelter and all other minimal needs needed for their survival, well-being and participation in society.

The second objective lies in ensuring that all of the world's poor people, including those who live in moderate poverty, get a chance and opportunity at climbing up the ladder of economic development.

In other words, we as a global society should see to it that the international rules governing the game in economic development does not intentionally or unintentionally set traps like protectionist trade barriers, insufficient development assistance, poorly designed rules and destabilization of global financial practices on the lower rungs of the ladder which only prevents the poor from climbing the rungs of economic development.

Millennium Development Goals (MDGs)

The dream of putting extreme poverty at hand is within our generation and reach through the bold set of commitments of Millennium Development Goals (MDGs) s, if and only if we grasp the historic opportunity available in front of us.

So far, the MDGs eight goals which were unanimously agreed and set by the largest gathering of world leaders in history, 191 UN members in September 2000 by signing the United Nations Millennium Declaration has halfway reached its target.

This is a set of 8 goals set to reduce poverty by half by the year 2015 with comparison to the baseline of 1990. Though the goals seem to be bold, they are achievable even though many countries have not achieved them so far. The rich countries promise to help the poorer countries reach these goals through improved global game rules and increased development assistance.

The eight MDGs goals are time-bound and quantified targets for the world to reach to address extreme poverty in various aspects- disease, hunger, absence of sufficient shelter, income poverty and omission while advocating gender equality, education and environmental viability. In addition to all this, there are the basic human rights or the rights for everyone on the planet to have access to shelter, security, health and education.

- The first goal is to eradicate extreme poverty and hunger.

- The second goal is to achieve universal primary education where both boys and girls everywhere should be able to complete a full course of primary school by 2015.

- The third goal promotes gender equality and empowers women by eliminating any gender disparity in both primary and secondary education preferably by 2005 and in all education levels no later than 2015.

- The fourth goal aims at reducing child mortality and consequently, the under-5 mortality number has reduced by two-thirds between 1990-2015.

- The fifth goal targets maternal health and consequently, the maternal mortality ratio has reduced by three quarters between 1990 and 2015.

- The sixth goal concentrates on combatting AIDS, malaria and other diseases and the spread of AIDS and HIV has been reversed.

- The seventh goal ensures environmental sustainability aims at reversing the loss of environmental resources by integrating sustainable development policies into country policies and programs.

- The eighth goal is to develop a global partnership for development through national and international open, rule-based and non-discriminatory trading and financial systems.

All this shows that the world has made significant progress in achieving most of the goals. The overall income level has increased by about 21% between 1990 and 2002 and the number of people in extreme poverty has reduced by about 130 million.

The number of child mortality rates have dropped from 103 per 1000 live births a year to only 88 deaths a year while the life expectancy age has increased from 63 to 65 years. Moreover, while an additional 8% of the world's population now have access to water, about 15% now have access to improved sanitation services.

The problem however is that this progress is not uniform across the world as there's huge disparities within countries. While poverty is greatest in rural areas, urban poverty is also extensive and growing unreported.

4. Poverty Transformations & Tested Methods

Poverty transformation is not something which can be done overnight, nor can it be completely eradicated. Poverty transformation or alleviation was made possible with the use of strategic tools like economic development, education, health and income redistribution. These tools help by improving the livelihoods of the world's poorest countries and also remove all the social and legal barriers to income growth amidst the poor. These tools include:

Education. With the help of quality education, people learn how and why they should make use of all the available opportunities around them. It is through knowledge and education that the children gain information and life skills they need to reach their goal and realize their potential.

To achieve this, the world needs to train quality teachers to impart all this training, build schools and the required infrastructure, provide the required education materials to the children and break down whatever inhibits or prevents children from accessing education.

Providing the necessary skills and training. By providing the youth and all those capable of working with farm work skills and other economic activities, they can finally start earning money to make a living and take care of their families. This is an absolute necessary in helping get rid of poverty as it is only if and when people realize and know how they can earn money can they fend for themselves and come out of their poverty.

Health, water and food. Many of the extremely poor children don't even have enough money for one meal a day, or for drinking water. Programs which provide food and water to the downtrodden feed hungry kids at school and also provide them with basic and necessary health services.

With these amenities available at school, parents automatically get encouraged to send their children to school for more reasons than one. Children who eat healthy meal are not only healthy, but also quickly learn and respond to the programme needs.

Income redistribution. By the redistribution of the country's wealth, the government can help develop the infrastructure of rural areas by providing them with roads, bridges and other economic facilities which make it easy to move goods, services and even farm produce to and from the different farming communities.

All it takes is the implementation of the above mentioned tools to see a marked improvement in the living conditions of the community. Pretty soon, things seem to be much better as poverty is slowly but surely eradicated from the extremely poor countries. In fact, all these pilot projects prove that all it takes is some intervention to bring about a positive change in these countries.

For example, it shows that so many lives can be saved in rural Africa only through antimalarial beds, it's possible to offer anti-AIDS drugs at affordable rates to the low-income group and that immunization can be arranged to be sent to the most difficult places of the world, even in a war zone.

This is proved in the following examples I have to give you on the fight against poverty. These examples show how some programs have been massively scaled up to affect an entire country or continent or even the world with great success.

1. Green revolution in Asia

The Asian green revolution can be considered one of the most important successes of targeted science over the century. It was the Rockefeller Foundation which took the initiative to start developing and promoting high varieties of staple crops first in Mexico and then in Asia. They started this out of fear of a possible massive hunger problem arising as a consequence of the rapidly growing population.

This started out in 1944 under the leadership of Dr. Norman Borlaug wherein crosses of strains were brought from Japan and scientifically bred to lead to a breakthrough. Since then, Mexico grew from a large importer of grains into a large grain exporter within 1964.

Not only did Borlaug then persuade donors to invest in similar cross-breeding, but also helped introduce the new scientific breeding technologies to local crop breeders to successfully develop new strains.

India thus grew from producing 11 million tons of wheat in 1960 to reducing 55 million tons in 1990, far surpassing the growth of the human population. Using the same basis and technology, more high-yield varieties were then developed for other crops and locations in various international institutions like the International Potato Center in Peru and International Rice Research Institute in Philippines.

2. Smallpox eradication

After claiming the lives of hundreds of millions of people through thousands of years of epidemics, it was a global effort which finally put an end to smallpox. Edward Jenner proving in 1976 that it was possible to use cowpox vaccine to prevent smallpox, formed the technological basis for its eventual eradication. While most of the rich were free from smallpox by the 1950s, it was still rampant in the poor countries where vaccine coverage was low.

In fact, smallpox infected about 10 to 15 million people in 1967 and claimed 1.5 to 2 million lives. This was when the World Health Organization started the Smallpox Eradication Unit and a mass worldwide vaccination with strong surveillance and containment. It was finally in 1980 that the WHO declared that the world was free from smallpox as the campaign had successfully reached all corners of the world including the impoverished regions of Asia and Africa.

3. Child survival campaign

James Grant, UNICEF"s executive director launched the Campaign for Child Survival in 1982. The campaign promoted GOBI interventions which included growth monitoring of children, oral rehydration therapy for diarrhea, breastfeeding for nutritional reasons and immunity diseases in infancy through immunization against six childhood killers; whooping cough, diphtheria, tuberculosis, tetanus, polio and measles.

This campaign too depended on the massively scaling up of standardized technologies in low-income settings wherein dozens of poor countries managed to conduct these campaigns while introducing these measures and make the immunization package reach at least 80% children.

This lead to striking results- there was a sharp drop in child mortality rates in all parts of the low-income world, including Africa which has the highest rates. In fact, the campaign helped save about twelve million lives by the end of the decade.

4. Global Alliance for Immunization and Vaccines

The campaign for childhood immunizations needed some fortifying by the late 1990s because of two reasons. The first was that there were many more immunizations that were developed and implemented in the rich countries but could not be implemented in poor countries because of its cost and lack of training and facilities.

Moreover, the coverage rates had depleted by the early 1990s mainly because of the intense poverty and economic crisis in Sub-Saharan Africa. This lead to Bill Gates accelerating and energizing the effort by announcing an initial gift of $750 million from the Bill and Melinda Gates Foundation and the launch of the Global Alliance for Vaccines and Immunizations in 2000.

After making as high as $1.1 billion commitments to the poor countries, the alliance managed to reach striking results of 41.6 million children getting vaccinated against hepatitis B, 3.2 million children vaccinated against yellow fever, 5.6 million children vaccinated against Haemophilus influenza type (Hib) and 9.6 million children vaccinated with other basic vaccines. Once again it was proven that it was the coupling of standardized technologies with mass distribution systems formed the base of the vaccination strategy for all proposals developed and submitted by recipient countries.

5. Malaria campaign

Though the many efforts launched by the World Health Organization in the 1950s and 1960s were adjudged a failure as malaria wasn't completely eradicated, the efforts were also considered a stunning success for those parts of the world where malaria was either eliminated or brought under control.

As a result of these efforts from WHO, more than half of the world's population living in the endemic regions were freed of malaria transmission and mortality in the 1940s, mainly in places where the control measures were favored by disease ecology. However Africa wasn't part of the program then or a beneficiary of its results today.

This regional successes were attributed to two standardized technologies. The use of DDT and other pesticides to reduce the disease's transmission and treating malaria cases using chloroquine and other new antimalarial drugs. In fact newer technologies of using antimalarial beds and combination therapies with DDT where required will reduce the malaria burden in Africa but not completely eradicate its transmission.

6. Bringing African River Blindness under control

It was in 1974 that the Onchocerciasis Control Program (OCP) was launched collectively by the Food and Agriculture Organization, World Bank, Merck, WHO and the United Nations Development Program to reduce the transmission of African river blindness or onchocerciasis. This is a disease transmitted by a black spy species and the program was launched in eleven hard-hit countries of West Africa.

The strategy used comprised of implementing various preventive measures like spraying airborne insecticides to reduce black flies and its treatment. When Merck and WHO scientists realized in the 1980s that a Merck drug used in veterinary medicine, ivermectin, was effective at treating African river blindness, Merck was ready to donate the drug on a large scale to help control the disease.

Consequently, OCP reports that their efforts not only lead to economic benefits, but also helped prevent about six hundred thousand cases of African river blindness, about forty million people were protected from the transmission of the disease and about twenty-five million hectares of land was considered safe for cultivation and settlement.

7. Polio eradication

Just like smallpox, it's possible to use immunization to globally eradicate polio. Though there are some technical differences between the two diseases, wherein polio is a bit more difficult to contain, its eradication is still possible, and will be achieved. The Global Polio Eradication Initiative was launched in 1988 by the World Health Assembly of the World Health Organization when polio was endemic in more than 125 countries.

However due to the massive efforts by various official institutions like WHO, UNICEF and US Centers for Disease Control and Prevention, the tireless efforts by Rotary International and actions in poor countries polio now remains and is contained only in six countries; Nigeria, Afghanistan, India, Pakistan, Niger and Egypt.

This is proven by the fact that only 784 cases were reported worldwide in 2003 which is a massive reduction when compared to the 350,000 cases reported in 1988. Moreover, since 1988 about two billion children have been immunized through the help of twenty million volunteers and $3 billion worth of international funding.

8. Propagation of family planning

There has been a massive drop in total fertility rates from an average of 5.0 children per woman in 1950 to 1955 to 2.8 children per woman in 1995 to 2000 with the introduction of modern contraception. This was all possible because of the family planning programs which provided advice and information, advocated the empowerment of women and promoted modern contraception.

Even other factors like urbanization, reduced child mortality, women's literacy and women's advent into the nonfarm work sphere have played a role. The coordination of all these efforts was managed by the United Nations Population Fund, which was established in 1969 and now operates in 140 countries.

Their efforts have led to a great increase in the use of modern contraceptives in couples in developing countries from 10-15% in 1970 to about 60% in 2000. Though the program is successful, there are some massive unmet needs because funds for contraceptive availability is much below the required levels in the poorest countries.

9. East Asian export processing zones

The Export Processing Zone or free trade zone has a great role to play in the early industrialization of East Asia after World War II. This is an industrial zone of a whole region or a country where special tax and infrastructure conditions are established to attract more foreign companies to set up their export-oriented manufacturing facilities.

It's basically established based on sufficient land for manufacturing operations, sufficient physical security in the zone, cheap proximity to an airport or seaport, tax holidays for profits and tax-free export of finished products and imports of inputs. These free-trade zones are responsible for East Asia's leap into the global production of toys, automotive components, footwear, garments and electronics and semiconductor markets.

Most of the time they started out with very low-skilled but high-labor operations like cutting and stitching of fabrics into ready-made garments and then progressed to higher technology aspects including product design. With this, the manufactured exports from East Asia rose at a rate of 12% per annum between 1978 and 2000 which is in dollars, $37 to $723 billion!

10. Bangladesh mobile phone revolution

Not only is Bangladesh's Grameen Bank famous for its microfinance lending, it is also famous for letting the world know about the expanded use of modern telecommunication in the poorest places. Grameen Telecom ventured into the mobile industry in 1997 and reached half a million subscribers by 2003, about their total number of landlines.

Its major achievement was the launching of a village phones program where a village woman borrows money to buy a mobile phone which is used through the village for a small charge. The collected charges is used by the woman for repaying her loan.

With Grameen's estimation of each phone reaching about 2,500 villagers, and with about 9,400 villages covered by early 2004, about 23 million villagers thus have access to a telephone. This is the same model now widely used in many other countries.

So if you take a close look, all these cases have common themes. The first proves that scaling up is possible only if and when it's backed by the right and widely applicable technology, financing and leadership.

Moreover in cases like smallpox and polio eradication, though the technologies had long existed, it hadn't been applied in the poorest settings. In cases like the Green Revolution's high-yield of food crops, the right technologies had to be developed and then targeted through a targeted effort.

However in practically all cases, technologies were adapted according to the local conditions like the maintaining of a 'cold chain' for immunizations which had to remain cold even in tropical settings and adapting the right crop-breeding technologies to the local climate, labor and land.

In case of MDGs the problem was that the promising technologies existed. The only problem was that it had not been scaled up yet, like antimalarial bed nets which are used by less than 1% of the rural Africans living in endemic, malaria regions.

This is why I believe, and support that social entrepreneurship is an absolute necessity to create positive changes in societies through different social initiatives.

5. What is social entrepreneurship?

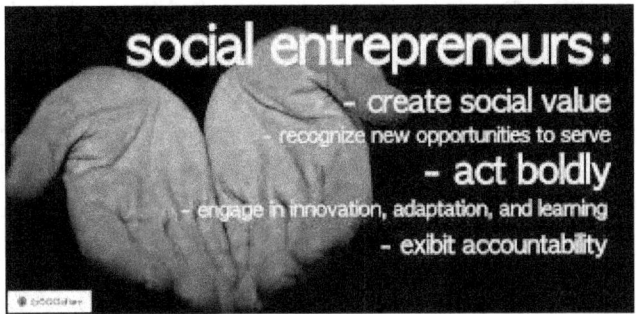

When you speak of social entrepreneurship, it revolves around recognizing the existing problems in society and then bringing about a social change through entrepreneurial principles, processes and operations.

It requires conducting some research about a particular social problem, and then organizing and creating the right social venture which can bring about the desired change. Of course, it's not necessarily that the change includes the total elimination of a social problem, and may include spending a lifetime focusing on improving existing social circumstances.

Social entrepreneurs use their entrepreneurship not only for commercial gains, but mainly to do some social good. J. Gregory Dees defines social entrepreneurship as the combination of a passion of a social mission with a business-like vision of innovation, discipline and determination.

Social entrepreneurship focuses on creating a social capital without calculating the performance in profit or monetary returns as social entrepreneurs are associated with non-profit sectors and organizations. They channel all their philanthropic energies into business ventures in the hope of creating values in business so that consumers eventually pay for goods and services wherein the social entrepreneur earns a profit which is then invested into the social ventures to bring about a positive change in society.

A social entrepreneur's program is targeted at the poor, underserved, neglected and basically highly disadvantaged population lacking the financial means or political contacts to bring about any transformation on their own. In short, it could be said that social entrepreneurs are builders to a better world. They are usually a part of, or are associated with some non-profit organizations (NGO) s.

Not only do social entrepreneurs focus on social problems, but they also focus on solving environmental problems like Child Rights Foundations, women empowerment foundations and plants for treating waste products. They are basically those people who are associated with non-profit and non-government organizations in raising funds through community events and activities.

While social entrepreneurship is a rather new term, and was conceptualized only a few decades back, it's been used throughout history. Many entrepreneurs have started social enterprises in a bid to eliminate social problems and in the process bring positive changes to society.

For example, Florence Nightingale was the founder of the first nursing school and developed modern nursing practices, Vinoba Bhave founded India's Land Gift Movement and Robert Owen was the founder of cooperative movement. They had established these organizations and foundations inn the19th century much before the introduction of social entrepreneurship in management. Today, the concept widely exists in various forms.

- Muhammad Yunus, the founder and manager of Grameen Bank is a social entrepreneur who was awarded the Nobel Peace Prize for his venture started in 2006. He pioneered the concept of microfinance and microcredit where loans are provided to poor entrepreneurs who do not and cannot qualify for a traditional loan. Till date, this venture has played a huge part in growing and benefiting a large section of the society.

- Rang De is another example of a non-profit social enterprise started by Ramakrishna and Smita Ram in 2008. It is an online platform where the poor in rural and urban India can access microcredits at an interest rate as low as 2% per annum. Lenders across India can lend money to borrowers, keep a track on their investments and also receive their regular payments online.

- Victoria Hale is another social entrepreneur who noticed that the poor couldn't access vital drugs as the profit-driven drug companies were not willing to develop drugs for the poor as they could not pay for them. Determined to do something about this, Hale founded the Institute for OneWorld Health, which is a nonprofit pharmaceutical company which ensures the poor can access vital drugs needed to treat infectious diseases, no matter what their ability to pay.

This is a one-of-its-kind institute which has recently acquired permission from the Indian government to use the drug paromomycin which cures visceral leishmaniasis, a disease killing more than 200, 00 annually.

While there are many other organizations who have brought about considerable change in the society, all these organizations work on the same principles of social entrepreneurship to address all the social problems so that they can improve the existing condition in society. Social entrepreneurship is growing in popularity and attracts numerous volunteers as it's a common term in university campuses.

It's growing so popular as the entrepreneurs consider it to be an outlet and means of doing whatever they have been thinking of for a long time. They work at transforming their brilliant ideas so that they bring about a change in society against all odds.

Social entrepreneurship is unlike entrepreneurship

While both entrepreneurs and social entrepreneurs pursue their dreams by starting new startups and initiatives, the entrepreneur's final aim is to make money. On the contrary, the social entrepreneur considers making money only a means to an end. In fact, they participate in profit making ventures only if they believe that the profits that are generated can be used to create some valuable social programs for the entire community.

There is an increasing need and demand for social entrepreneurs today as the current international economic crisis is aggravating the exiting social problems like poverty and unemployment. This is why J. Gregory Dees believes that social entrepreneurship is needed to cushion the financial consequences on the weakest in the society.

The financial burdens will lead to fewer people receiving proper health care, fewer children attending school as parents cannot bear the burden of formal education and tension and violence increases as the poor compete amongst each other for jobs and money making opportunities. All this leads to a drop in progress as those who had come out of poverty fall back into it.

This also leads to a tightening of household, government and business budgets wherein expensive environmental protection and clean up endeavors all end up in jeopardy. As environmental and social issues are time sensitive, not recognizing the need and importance of social entrepreneurship, and not supporting such efforts in this downturn is a serious mistake.

Characteristics of a social entrepreneur

Not everyone is or can become a social entrepreneur. It could be said that they are born and destined to become social entrepreneurs as there are some specific characteristics which make them. These characteristics are:

- They can be called social catalysts as they have visions to create some fundamental social changes by reforming the existing social systems and creating sustainable social improvements. J. Gregory Dees says that though they act locally, their actions can stimulate global improvements in particular areas like education, economic development, health care, the arts, the environment or practically any other social field.

- They are socially aware people who knows what problems the society if going through. This is why their ultimate goal of their programs is not profit but social improvement. In fact, their endeavors' success is not measured based on the amount of profits it generated but on the social impact it creates.

- They are always looking for opportunities. They look at an obstacle not as a hindrance, but consider it to be a point they had missed in their plans, and learn from the obstacle and the method used to overcome it to improve and fine-tune their business goals.

- Social entrepreneurs are not followers. They are innovative and creative and tend to think outside of the box. They are always ready to apply new ideas to new situations and take it as a challenge as they know not all innovations end up successful. They readily accept failures and are in fact mentally ready for them as they know that failures are stepping stones to success.

- They are resourceful by nature which is why they don't let their existing resources limit their visions and goals. In fact, instead of falling back because of limited resources, they know how to, and work at optimizing their existing resources by collaborating their resource pool with others.

- They're accountable to their beneficiaries and to themselves. They keep on asking themselves if they are heading in the right direction and if they understand their people's needs.

  They need to know and assure themselves that they are creating something valuable and useful to the people they serve. Moreover, they know, and accept the fact that they are accountable to their investors who want to know how much and well their contributions are stimulating social improvements as projected and promised by the social entrepreneurs.

Social entrepreneurship is not charity work

Charity and social entrepreneurship are two different entities not to be confused with. Charity is something which reflects the benefactor's love for humankind. It is measured based on their generosity to the less fortunate.

On the contrary, social entrepreneurship brings out more of their good intentions where these intensions are not driven by compassion but are instead compelled with a wish or desire to create a social change.

This is why charitable establishments have to depend on their donors' contributions which is not constant but changes with the economic climate. However non-profit organizations practicing social entrepreneurship do not depend much on donor funds as they survive on their self-sustaining social programs. Social entrepreneurs in other words don't just spend, but invest the donor contributions they receive in social ventures which can generate enough revenue to sustain themselves.

This is why those who do charity work only use the donor funds they receive to buy food to ease the poor's hunger or medicine to cure a health problem. This only provides temporary relief. On the contrary, social entrepreneurs use their funds wisely by creating instructional programs teaching the poor things like how to grow their own food so that they don't go hungry, and can take care of themselves in the long run.

They show them work opportunities to earn money to fend themselves and thus buy any medication they require for treatment. So in today's world of scarce resources, it's no longer enough to just donate food or money for good intentions. Your donations also have to create a social impact on the masses.

Social entrepreneurs don't just make donations or charity work to provide for a temporary solution. They work at identifying all the opportunities which have the potential and capabilities of changing the world. They identify and implement programs which help generate massive and lasting solutions to the world's biggest problems.

Social entrepreneurship and innovation

Social entrepreneurs should be ready to toy around and be innovative and ready to tread in places no one has ventured into before. As they work in different contexts throughout their career where each situation requires a new solution, they have to be flexible with their approach and thinking. Social innovations thus includes means, ways, strategies, ideas and even organizations which think of innovative solutions to meet the public needs, especially the poverty ridden.

These innovations can include various setups like healthcare, community development and education and are created to better not only one person or community, but the entire society. While all social innovations may not be successful, failures are considered as blessings in disguise as social entrepreneurs learn and thus know what to avoid in future endeavors.

It is when the social venture achieves its intended social impact that it is deemed successful. The following methodologies help at ensuring the venture ends up a successful one.

The mission statement captures the impact and should thus be short and specific. Examples are 'the poor will earn more money' or 'fewer will get or die of malaria' while statements like 'improving lives' and 'fighting injustice' are two vague.

The social entrepreneur then assesses and finds out if the social program justifies the mission statement by collecting concrete statistical data. In case of 'poor earning more money', the income information of the families before and after the innovation has to be collected and analyzed to quantitatively measure the impact. The social entrepreneur may have to find a suitable metric to capture results with integrity if the impact is varied and complex.

Just measuring the impact is not enough; the social entrepreneur also has to prove that it was the social program which produced the desired changes. This can be achieved by conducting scientific randomized trials using control groups to study the correlation between a specific social innovation and the social changes. One can also depend on past studies of similar programs which were conducted by other researches or social entrepreneurs to provide concrete evidence justifying the social endeavors' efficacy.

Cost-effective

As funding is limited in social initiatives, it's required to keep track of the amount of donor money needed to create an impact. Social entrepreneurs should be cost-effective and know how to optimize each dollar to produce maximum benefits to the beneficiary. It's also important to evaluate and determine if the program will be cost-effective over time.

As cost-effectiveness is relative, it's better to compare the project with some other projects meant to produce similar effects. If there's nothing to compare with, at least ensure the effectiveness seems reasonable and can be measured.

Sustainability

It's also important to consider if the social initiative is sustainable in the long run. The initial positive impact of an effective program does not fade away but continues to generate benefits even with scarce funding. For a social program to have a sustainable impact, it needs one or more of the following characteristics:

The project produces a self-sustaining community process which provides a solution to a local problem without any external funding. The project should leave a business model and supply chain which continues to provide the required goods and services at a profit.

While it's possible to hand over the goods or services to the local government which collects taxes to fund the program, this is not always a viable option as it's not sustainable to rely on the government. Lastly, the project has to permanently get rid of the problem it tries to solve either by getting rid of the problem itself or by causing a permanent change.

The Grameen Bank's microcredit system is a perfect model of sustainability. Muhammad Yunus had lent $27 of his personal funds to a group of poor women to start a sewing machine through which they generated sufficient money to repay the loan and rise above poverty. The bank thus sustains itself by charging interest in its loans and then recycling its capital amount to help other women.

Social entrepreneurship in developing countries

Unfortunately social entrepreneurs in developing countries go unrecognized not because of a lack of talent, but just because the projects they'd initiated to lift themselves out of poverty just go unrecognized.

Only MBAs and investments bankers are usually recognized for social entrepreneurship for their specialized training in an institution. It is however time that poor people who become social entrepreneurs get recognized for their efforts in improving their lives and the lives of people around them.

A survival technique for the poor

Most of the time, social entrepreneurship is a necessity for the poor to eke out a living. They have low or even no visibility in the field as they do not engage in public relations and have no language skills or resources like internet for exposure.

Nevertheless, they make significant contributions for the improvement of their communities. While their initiatives may not go large scale, they do create a huge impact on their immediate surroundings and the poor people around them.

Unlike popularly believed, most people prefer creating a sustainable means of living instead of living on charity. It is once they generate a consistent income for their and their family's financial security, they start using their skills to serve others through their social ventures.

Localities as social entrepreneurs

It is assumed that foreigners initiate most social ventures because they think something should be done to solve a social problem. However localities don't rely on their initiatives; they instead take the initiative to develop their own initiatives to tackle the social issues. Their knowledge of their immediate surroundings, needs and their experience gives them an added advantage to take action.

However, the social initiative works out better if the local entrepreneur's talent is collaborated with the work of social entrepreneurs from developed countries as they can provide the necessary funding and other resources. One of the resources they can offer for social entrepreneurship is technology, and I have explained its impact on the market and poverty in the forthcoming chapter.

6. How can technology revolutionize market

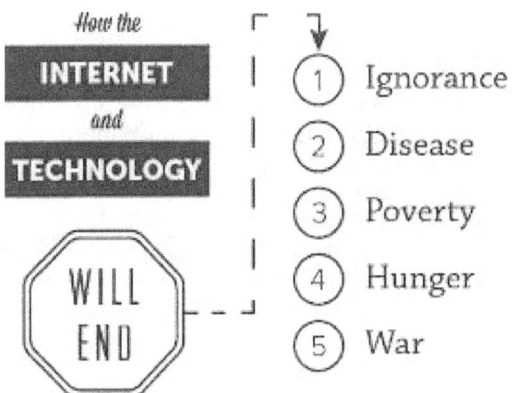

Technology has an important role in social entrepreneurship as technology is not only innovative, but is increasingly becoming cost effective at deploying technology to help solve various social issues and problems.

In fact, just having access to modern information and communications technology (ICT) helps increase socioeconomic development. Not only access, even what people do with access to technologies like email, community radio, internet and mobile telephone leads to greater socioeconomic development.

This is better understood if the three words 'information and communications technology' are clearly defined. With access to information, people can make informed decisions benefiting both their professional and personal lives. It should be accessible to people who understand it, and the target group of consumers and those generating information has to increase the accessibility of information where unavailable.

It is through communication that people join their forces, discuss and share views and ideas and also work at co-creating solutions which help them take care of their own problems. New forms of communication has to be built and not replace the traditional forms like radio, television, meetings and fixed telephones.

Technology helps to quickly access, gather and spread information and lets people communicate faster and more efficiently. So ICT can be used to accelerate the eradication of poverty by not only promoting economic opportunities but also by creating awareness and empowerment. Unfortunately the developing countries do not benefit much from modern ICT as internet access is still expensive and unreliable in most developing countries. That's why its user rates is still below 5% in rural areas of Africa and Latin America.

However mobile phone use is spreading in Africa and Latin America faster than the internet. In fact, while mobile phone penetration in developed countries exceeds 100 subscriptions per 00 inhabitants, it's 58.2 subscriptions per 100 inhabitants in developing countries.

Unfortunately, despite this rapid expansion of mobile services, less than 5% is used for business or development purposes. It's not enough to just have internet access and mobile phones for social development.

The farmer in Uganda and health worker in Mali should know where and how to find relevant information and connect with others. So ICT success depends on its overall progress in reaching the MDGs in relation to the spread of these technologies.

Related to innovative processes

ICT should be related to innovative processes which address all the social problems existing in developing countries. It should help professionals like health workers and teachers work better and help farmers change their livelihood. ICT should help them grow more effective and efficient in their work and help them connect to more people through their networks.

So for example, to the farmer living in the mountains who can't move to a less isolated place has better access to information through technology and the internet and phones. They get connected to diverse people and need not depend on people around him to make better decisions.

Similarly in the education sector, social innovation helps the young living in sparsely populated areas with limited amenities have better career opportunities as distance education helps them learn despite there not being any training courses in their neighborhood. Moreover, social innovation leads to the development of new services which generate better paid local jobs.

In the health sector, social innovation creates a new mindset about using traditional treating methods because of better information. Even rural hospitals usually located in remote areas have a better chance of employing highly skilled medical workers through ICT. They also have more possibilities to connect and exchange information with peers and can learn just by consulting other medical specialists.

Better education helps farmer negotiate for better prices and teaches them better methods to grow more crops. Better education provides improved healthcare in remote areas to give healthy and skilled workforce and more self-employed people and jobs. All this work at eradicating poverty.

Effects of applying ICT to agriculture, health, education and economic development

ICT improving agricultural livelihoods and economy

With ICT intervening in a country's economic development kit helps producers increase their individual and group income level and employment opportunities to help eradicate poverty. ICT can be used for:

Providing access to market and price information

Individual producers and entrepreneurship organizations like cooperatives and unions can negotiate and bargain better if they have access to market and price information. The combined use of the internet, radio and mobile phones let producers negotiate higher prices and earn more. It also provides access to information related to quality management, product and certification tracking and tracing the production process.

ICT also helps organizations gain regular access to input and production methods for increasing productivity and consequent income levels. More concentration is placed on providing information to female entrepreneurs and additional measures are taken to ensure women can also access program's skills.

ICT helps entrepreneurs and organizations improve their business skills which helps provide better employment opportunities to youths and service providers. All this helps reduce poverty amidst both male and female youths and adults.

ICT improving access and quality of education

There are five aspects of the education sector which ICT application affects.

1. **Efficacy-** ICT helps improve the management and administration of schools and governing bodies by streamlining information and providing quick and easy access to information.

2. **Teaching methods**: ICT helps teachers revolutionize their teaching methods using digitalized learning materials. The use of multimedia in classrooms make studding and lessons more interesting, and easier for pupils to follow. It also makes it easier to perform scientific experiments in cases where facilities and equipment are missing like in physics.

Of course, to benefit from the teachers' newly acquired ICT skills, they have to first be given training in pedagogical skills which helps them bring out the best in online and offline teaching articles and tools.

3. **Education material quality:** With ICT, teachers no longer need to teach using substandard and outdated learning materials. They can use the internet and multimedia to develop their own teaching materials by finding internet sources to update their existing teaching materials and using multimedia to present all this in a more attractive and interactive format to their pupils. Consequently, the new learning materials can be distributed and made more accessible to pupils both offline and online.

4. **Computer literacy:** With youths receiving training at school and vocational training centers in computer proficiency and maintenance and repair, their acquired computer skills improves their job chances and prepares them for the 21st century knowledge-based economy.

5. **Access to education:** People living in remote areas with few schools and training centers can receive decent education or vocational training through distance education.

With ICT intervention in the education sphere, teachers in primary, secondary and vocational training centers have better learning opportunities fitting their needs. This provides an increased quality and equity in the education system.

ICT improving healthcare access and quality

ICT can help improve the health sector in various ways and particularly in:

- **Improving efficiency and effectiveness:** With many of the world's health systems unable to reach the poor, ICT helps improve their access to and efficiency of health services. This in turn helps in streamlining process and making information transparent and easily accessible.

  The digitizing of important information like administration of patient records and stock supplies not only saves the health workers' precious time, but also provides hospital managers with valuable management information to run the hospital effectively and efficiency. Government officials also benefit with access to timely and accurate data at their fingertips as it helps them plan better and prepare for health policies.

- **Telemedicine and continued medical education:** ICT improves the delivery and access to healthcare services in inaccessible regions. Healthcare professionals use ICT to exchange information with medical specialists using audio-conferencing, personal digital assistants and CD-ROMs for a better diagnosis, treatment and prevention of diseases and injuries. Moreover, healthcare professionals can easily continue their education via the internet by following online courses and accessing the latest medical research information.

ICT is especially useful for community-based organizations employing health workers and caregivers as it helps people gain access to required health services.

ITC and economic development

The use of ICT to support productivity and market information in low-income countries helps farmers and entrepreneurs make better decisions and thus increase their income and opportunities for employment.

However the main problem affecting ICT's success in most countries like Ghana, Mali and Ethiopia is the lack of organizational development amidst producers and entrepreneurial organizations. In more developed countries with organized producers like Ecuador, Peru and Zambia, there is an opportunity to use more advanced ICT applications to expand the export market and help with certification of products.

In case of Latin America, ICT can be used for supporting financial services, especially those having increased access to financial services through the use of mobile service providers. This helps improve the quality of, and access to financial services.

Factors which can limit ICT success

Accessibility

One of the problems developing countries face about implementing new technologies is though they are willing to implement new technologies for economic growth and human development, they do harbor fears about how the internet and mobile phones may end up being used for criminal purposes or to undermine the powers in place.

They fear that the sudden influx of connection technologies may threaten the status quo as most of these countries have weak or failed central governments, young, unskilled and unemployed populations and underdeveloped economies.

These countries are however ready to import and use connection technologies as they recognize the potential its potential for creating sustainable economies. They however have to take a strong political stand to let the dramatic changes of access to connectivity get implemented. Moreover, in some cases, accessibility may just be another political challenge.

Another factor which falters accessibility to ICT is the availability of energy for the ICT structure. To help overcome this problem, an increasing number of ICT infrastructure solutions are today used with an adapted energy source like solar or generator to ensure its energetic independence.

Various forms of ICT can provide solutions to reach out to more poor users. It could involve using computer databases for analytical power and centralizing knowledge before distributing the requested information through widely diffused ICT like community radio and mobile phones. This thus shows that mobile telephony, PCs, radio and the Internet are all complementary and not competing solutions for providing information and communication.

Affordability

Affordability of ICT is another major challenge to overcome as affordability is important to help enable ICT to be a motor for change. It's only if these services are affordable can the poor people benefit from greater access to the services.

As it is known that ICT can help eliminate poverty by letting poor men and women build livelihood assets or secure more employment opportunities, these new technologies can make a difference if implemented even in the most remote places. This is why new micro-enterprises in various sectors have been started to produce more and new ways to market technology related goods like the Bangladesh mobile phone revolution.

ICT and its role in social development

Not only is ICT used as a tool to improve social efficiency, it also is a key factor for improvements in various environments which support new processes to facilitate increased transparency and efficiency. It has an instant impact on people using it in both a concrete and direct way. It democratizes information flow to make the intersection and leveling of local and global spheres possible through radio to mobile phones.

ICT helps reduce the gap between growth producers and subsistence producers where subsistence producers produce food mainly to feed their own families. They don't sell to the global market to make a profit as they are not only overlooked in the formal global economy, they have trouble benefiting from measures and opportunities which help improve their production yields and consequent incomes. With access to relevant information and credit, subsistence farmers can become growth producers.

Moreover, coalitions and networks are important for successful and long-lasting changes as innovation is possible if there is interaction between people. This is where ICT has an important part in facilitating networks and bringing people together. It helps support the development of resilient businesses and social entrepreneurship in developing countries.

For example, before the advent of the email, you had to write, print or type hundred letters and post them if you had to contact hundred people. However because of technology and the internet, all you now need to do is use one email message to reach 100s of people.

All you need to do is customize the headers and names of the people you have to send the message to and then everyone is efficiently and effortlessly reached with a single click of the mouse. Moreover you can use email to reach anyone anywhere in the world without having to pay for postage and incur additional expenses.

Similarly, such technology proves very helpful to an underprivileged person who's starting out on her or his own venture. The entrepreneur can reach a global audience using mobile and internet technologies to not only increase the scale aspect but also offer a cheaper solution creating more value per unit of cost basis.

So all this proves that if technology is harnessed and used properly it can indeed help revolutionize the market. by providing those living in poverty access to technologies like electricity, technology which provides clean water, technology which improves agricultural yield, technology which helps improve access and type of education and healthcare and technology which helps prepare for natural disasters, these people grow more efficient and come out of poverty and start earning money.

Instead of depending on charity, technology helps the poor learn to fend for themselves so that they can become independent and earn for themselves while doing something or the nation. In fact, all you need is a some minimal investment and your self-learning to start and implement any technology idea you may have. I'll delve more into this in the next chapter.

7. How to start your technology idea with minimum investment and self-learning

Technological ideas, if implemented properly, can go a great way into eradicating poverty by helping the poor earn money and fend for themselves. This independence is much better than depending on charity all the time. So if you have a technology idea you think and know will help the poor, you now have to start and implement it using the following ideas and strategies.

You however need to know that with your idea and its unique opportunities come the many problems and obstacles which may challenge the fundamentals of your idea. You basically need to know what and which new technologies should be brought into the market with minimal investment and training.

This is not something you can do alone. Though some research may help you in this direction, it's also better if you acquire some help from payroll outsourcing companies who will be able to help you with your startup business. Basically, if you have a technology startup in mind, here is a quick guide showing you how you can start your business.

Do some research

You need to first do some research about the timelines and feasibility about the technology you plan to implement and pioneer through your social entrepreneurship. Start by writing down what you think the problem your startup will be solving. If you write this down, you are constantly reminded about that problem, and you in fact get more and better ideas you can use to tackle the problem.

Next you need to determine the extremities of this problem, and how many people are actually suffering from the problem. Think of some questions and ask them their views about your thoughts and ideas. Once you have collected sufficient data, compare it with the competitors to find out if you are doing something different and unique enough to compete with them. Keep all the researched data some place safe as it could prove useful in securing needed funding later on.

At times, a competitor is not enough for success; in fact, the lack or absence of a competitor may indicate that the technology or idea you plan to implement is not actually ready or ripe for the market as yet. In such a situation, if you are startup for financial gains, it's better waiting for a while. However if you plan to implement something new which the economy and society lacks and greatly requires, it's better to go ahead with the risk and trust your intuition.

Take a look at your financial standing

It is not cheap pioneering a technology startup, or even just enhancing any existing one. You need money as it's rather expensive, especially if you require lots of infrastructure and manpower to implement it. This is why before you move forward, you need to first take a look at your financial capabilities.

You need to be financially and mentally prepared for a lean period in the first few months of your endeavor. This is because in most of the cases, all technology businesses start with losses without their actually seeing or tasting any positive profit.

However, don't lose heart if you are not financially capable or stable to start your venture. There are many interested investors and joint venture capitalists who are more than ready to invest in new technologies and ideas which benefit and help the society, especially those in need.

If you plan to make use of this investment money, you first need to produce a detailed and well-researched business marketing plan to attract and rope in the right venture capitalists for your venture.

Rope in the right people for your team

It's not actually possible for anyone to implement an idea on their own. So if you decide, and accept the fact that you can't do the investment, marketing and other aspects of the business on your own, you need to get the right people to help you do it.

Don't think that your lack in any skill like marketing or technology is a hindrance to your technology business success. You need to have the right people on your team so that they can provide you with the best investment and skills to get the job done. In fact, if you surround yourself with the right people, it forms the basis and key to the success of your, or any business.

Choose the right location for your startup

This is important as the place you work has an effect on your startup as you get off the ground. It is mainly because different environments offer different working styles; you need to choose and work from a place with suits your working and thinking style.

Most of the time, startup founders prefer working from home as it saves them money and unnecessary expenses. Then again, there are also some people who prefer renting a co-working place wherein they share an office for the startup. However though you shouldn't be afraid to experiment while starting your business, you also shouldn't let the search for the perfect locality get in your way of work.

Set your goals right

Setting a goal is very important for any business venture. No business will last long or succeed if you don't have any goals created and set for it. Chalk out your goals based on all the market research you had done earlier, and all the collected data. You then have to go on pursuing them based on the fundamentals of your marketing plan, which may change as you reach each goal.

However whatever changes, you need to be ready for them by keeping both short and long term goals. This way you can make alterations to your plan as per the consequences of these goals for the long time benefit and success of your technology business. Don't stop setting goals as these goals provide the motivation for you to move forward in your venture. It is based on these goals that you will be able to determine your actions and the steps you need to take to reach your goals.

Branding

Branding does not involve just choosing a name for your venture. It is about deciding and choosing an identity to give your idea. Not only should you choose something you love, but you also need to decide and choose a name which effectively conveys the experience of using your product and the problem it is meant to solve.

However you need to choose your name wisely. You need to look around for any existing product which has either succeeded or failed, and is associated with any name you have chosen. Examine it to find out what impact it has on adoption.

This is when you need to secure your website name and other related marketing materials, and craft out your elevator pitch so that you know what to say to anyone who asks for information about your company.

Incorporation

Incorporation is the process of legalizing your startup entity and deciding on its structure. Startups are usually incorporated as an LLC, S corporation or C corporation where LLCs and S corporations have special tax exemptions while C corporations are taxable entities. Incorporation is important for a startup as there are various aspects of the startup lifecycle it affects, and gets affected by it.

Besides tax differences, there are other considerations to bear in mind while incorporating like equity compensation which is important when raising capital and based on your chosen business structure. You also need to decide where you want to incorporate as different states and countries have different ways of taxing businesses.

Find a co-founder

You need the right support for your endeavor to move forward and succeed. In fact, this is why many investors place emphasis, and first look for the right founding team before considering the idea. Of course, if you already know or have a co-founder, well and fine. However if you don't, you need to look for the right person.

You need to look for someone who not only has a solid track record, but also whom you have some history with. The main thing you need to look out for is a person who has a skill set which complements your skills.

The person you choose should also have a style and personality which matches yours as you will both be working together for a long time and should be compatible enough to accomplish goals as a team.

It is very important to remember that in most startups, there is only room for one person to be in the limelight. So there is a chance that one of you will have to work behind the scenes, and both of you should be ready and comfortable with it.

Create and follow a calendar

Now that you have your goals set right, you need to have a detailed description and calendar of all the tasks that have to be accomplished in the time span, and the equipment you will need to buy during the implementation period.

This is important as this calendar helps you anticipate your working costs and expenses, helps you avoid any possible delays and also minimizes all the interruptions to your work processes. So you need to keep a tab on the calendar and your work to maximize your productivity and minimizing interruptions with your technology startup plan.

8. Social Entrepreneurship in Developed V/s Developing Countries

Now we know that entrepreneurship is global force which generates jobs, growth and competitiveness in countries. However you, or anyone for that matter, may wonder if entrepreneurs in developing countries face more problems with their venture than entrepreneurs in developed countries. So here is a 'discussion' about how entrepreneurship progresses in developed and developing countries.

There is a marked difference in social entrepreneurship in developing and developed countries and it is by understanding this difference that you can expect and enforce private sector development in developing countries.

The inefficiency of markets in most developing countries is one such difference; however the response entrepreneurs give to these inefficiencies is rather surprising and counterintuitive. There are three important distinctions between entrepreneurship in developed and developing countries- opportunity, financial resources and apprenticeship and human resources.

In fact, the wealth and poverty in developing countries is linked to the entrepreneurial nature of the country's economics. Countries with more entrepreneurship, see a marked growth in economic growth, competitiveness and innovation, and may also have an important part in poverty alleviation.

Despite all this, unfortunately, the entrepreneurship in developing countries is the least studied social and economic phenomenon today. While there are over 400 million people who are owners or managers of new firms in developing countries, there are only 18 million such entrepreneurs in the US. Moreover, of the 400 million, 200 million are located in India and China alone.

Why entrepreneurs in developing countries are different

The entrepreneurs in developing countries have distinct characteristics. Some of them help improve the chances of any success in growth-oriented firms while others unfortunately tend to hold back these firms. Take a look at these three attributes which distinguish entrepreneurs in developing countries from those in developed countries.

Opportunity

The entrepreneurs in developing countries have more opportunities than those in developed countries. It is these opportunities which help and allow firms to follow a portfolio approach for a strategy which efficiently manages higher business levels and market risk. In fact, entrepreneurs in developing countries have different circumstances if compared to their counterparts in developed countries. These differences are attributed to the economics they operate by.

The entrepreneurs in emerging markets don't have a mature market offering the consistency these markets are known for. Moreover, entrepreneurship in emerging markets is rather pervasive. While entrepreneurs who startup in the developed countries tend to operate at the economy fringes, entrepreneurs in developing countries operate closer to the core as the needs and opportunities available here are more widespread.

While entrepreneurs in developing countries face a reduced competitive threat from their well-established counterparts, their economic, political and regulatory uncertainty is increased and may at times even outweigh direct competitive threats.

This is why the rational but sometimes counter intuitive response especially from those trained in western business strategy is that entrepreneurs in developing countries need to spread their resources across various separate but related businesses as it helps mitigate all systematic risks. This means that entrepreneurs who operate in segmented markets, which are popular in developing countries, have a surrogate role as a financial investor who manages all risks through portfolio diversification.

In other words, the entrepreneur manages portfolio risk by managing various businesses on behalf of investors who would otherwise do the same. With not many alternative finance sources, successful entrepreneurs may use internally generated cash of one business to fund other businesses.

Some examples of this system are the keiretsu system in Japan and chaebols in Korea. These systems comprise of interlocking ownerships and business partnerships which were developed this way. Not only do interlocked businesses provide a source of funding and reduces risks, they also provide a source of informal information flow, access to more manpower with more skills and resources and also when it is well implemented, it creates a brand name to use across all businesses.

Now one wonders if and when interlocking business conglomerates like this are so common amidst the entrepreneurs in developing countries, how did they start in the first place? Well, it's usually bad access to capital and a fragmented retail and distribution system which makes entrepreneurs start businesses downstream where they have direct access to their end customer.

When they start downtown, they have reduced initial capital requirements as their working capital is reduced while they have access to customers and information source which is frequently lacking. Not many realize the importance of access to such information, and it is often overlooked as a key success factor.

So while they have achieved success in retail and distribution, successful entrepreneurs tend to leverage their domain experience, the cash flow generated and information flow wherein they can integrate vertically and move into their upstream businesses.

Finance

It is a fact that entrepreneurs in developing countries have broader opportunities with resultant strategies that are naturally self-hedging. However an absence of financial innovation and restricted personal and family savings greatly reduces the growth prospects of all the innovative and potential startups in developing countries.

In fact, the nature of the entrepreneurship in developing countries affect their entrepreneurial finance in these countries. More than in developed countries, entrepreneurs here in developing countries have to answer some financial questions to avail financial help.

They have to answer questions like: if there are less than 50% odds of the new enterprise surviving its first 5 years, it is logical or imperative for an entrepreneur to commit their own or someone else's financial resources to a new firm? If no, what is the reason for the increased tendency of entrepreneurs starting new businesses? How is it actually logical to finance businesses which have an odds of success that is less than that of a coin toss?

So internal finance constitutes most of the financing for small and medium enterprises in most developing countries. Entrepreneurs rely on these funding sources, which provide 87% to 100% of the outside capital raised by entrepreneurs. So other financial institutions have a small role in financing entrepreneurs in the startup stage.

Not many understand how potential entrepreneurs actually accumulate the necessary capital to start a business. The question of how they actually save funds from their own sources of income to start a business comes to mind, especially if quite a modest amount is required.

Accordingly, there are now two issues to be discussed -the source of income and the appropriate places to keep the money safe till the new business is started. The sources of income are varied and may include savings from a previous salary and in some cases where they are well paid, entrepreneurs may also save their startup capital from their salaries.

Research has proven that developing countries which have undergone economic instability usually have more private savings. To them, crisis leads to opportunity where it's necessary to form large pools of private capital to start a business. Moreover, with successful entrepreneurship being associated with urbanization, urbanization leads to increased individual expenses and a consequent reduction in private savings.

This is why successful entrepreneurs tend to work at saving more money in the countryside so that they have money to start their business. This leads to the development of family networks spanning both to the urban and rural areas. However how private rural savings are later converted into urban entrepreneurship is not well understood, and may be different in different countries.

Statistically, microenterprises too contribute in creating a pool of savings through which larger and more sophisticated enterprises are launched. However limited attractive savings mechanisms, and negative real interest rates on bank deposits in both formal and informal financial sectors and the difficulties associated with investing in land or some real estate has severely reduced savings.

The absence of secure premises is also limited because of other forms of de facto savings like inventory accumulation. These are the main reasons why microenterprises don't serve as launching pads for entrepreneurships, especially the growth-oriented ones, in developing countries.

One last overlooked, and frequently undocumented development is the rising consumerist nature of economies in developing countries which has led to a drop in personal savings rate and a growth in personal consumer-related indebtedness. This growth in personal indebtedness may in turn constrain the entrepreneur's willingness and capacity to start a new firm in some countries like North Africa and Middle East.

The established new firms in many developing countries use various unconventional techniques for their finance. As the financial markets in these countries are rather underdeveloped, bootstrap financing is rather predominant form of early stage financing here. So now comes the question why outside formal finance sources, especially risk capital finance forms needed by new growth-oriented entrepreneurs are not available in large numbers.

One of the most important reasons could be that the macroeconomic conditions in growing markets contradict the high IRRS required by investors for risk compensation. So though there are no statistics on private equity investing in growing markets, IRRs practically breakeven for the first generation of such funds. Consequently, these returns are not enough to attract large investors into the next generation risk capital vehicles.

However risk capital finance is important for growth-oriented entrepreneurs in developing countries as it aligns the incentives of outside investors and entrepreneurs. Each works at maximizing the enterprise's economic value instead of one person's loss being compensated by the other's gain at the other's expense. Zero-sum games are however common between commercial lending banks and entrepreneurs in developing countries.

Unfortunately, while risk capital finances is important in the entrepreneurial procedure in developed countries, it hasn't reached its full potential in developing countries. Though the American venture capital mode has limited applications in this market, it is usually first approached by fund managers concentrating on developing countries.

These venture capital funds work only with few companies which in turn constricts their development impact. Both venture capital and private equity funds cannot exit most of their investments because of the liquidity of local stock markets in developing countries.

The successful venture capitalists have rare skills acquired through experience and not through education and training. This in turn restricts the number of risk capital organizations which can be organized. Moreover, today's risk capital finance requires that new institutions are set up before starting its investment operations which slows the investment process and in most cases, makes it difficult to invest funds in the investment cycle.

So how is it possible to overcome these hurdles? Though there has been a revolution in the developed capital markets over the past 50 years, not much innovation has made its way to entrepreneurial firms in developing countries.

For example, income-linked loans, loans which are repaired through the borrower's future income, was first introduced to finance higher education in US but was later applicable to all types of borrowers including the entrepreneurial firms in developing countries. Consequently, lenders like commercial banks, fund managers, non-bank financial institutions and others offered long-term loans spanning 10 years or more to entrepreneurial borrower.

These loans were repaid by the firm's future income and some index of aggregate incomes which could include borrowers from the same field in a region like all Indonesian garment manufacturers, borrowers from any field but in the same geographic region like Brazilian borrowers, or a combination of the two.

Human resources and apprenticeship

Global competitive firms need to be created with some industry-specific training as these firms usually form into geographically focused industrial clusters. This is proven through the emergence of globally competitive industries in developing countries like India's software cluster, Philippines's animation outsourcings cluster and China's wireless market.

This clustering concept is however not of much use to entrepreneurial opportunities in markets where there are no essential preconditions. In fact, it's not construed if clustering is actually a precondition for creating globally competitive firms in developing countries.

Moreover, it's not easy operating in developing markets without mentors and normal avenues of preparation. It's even more difficult operating in mal-developed or corrupt economies as the leading companies here are not always the best guides for new businesses. Businesses also find it difficult reaching certain scales without the right skill sets like financial management.

Entrepreneurship is also difficult to succeed without the necessary mentorship and apprenticeship. While developed countries like Silicon Valley have lots of talent, marquee companies serving as informal finishing schools and a culture which encourages innovation and new businesses, entrepreneurship and apprenticeship can be developed together without all this.

At an elementary level, even the most basic business training and local support groups of like-minded entrepreneurs can help increase business success rates and repayment of micro lending organizations. However not many of these enterprises reach regionally competitive levels in national or global levels.

At a more professional level in developed countries, multinationals serve as training grounds for prospective entrepreneurs. However as the multinationals' foreign direct investment is related to the general business environment, and as apprenticeship in firms is important for entrepreneurship, these observations have to be compared with the lack of connectivity between entrepreneurs and the general business environment.

The successful entrepreneurship activities usually have local businessmen as mentors and outside advisors. However as the business grows, corporate governance slowly overtakes mentorship for guidance wherein a group of savvy local businessmen and local or international industry experts have a crucial role in the expansion stage.

While the developing countries need revolutionary changes, only a few people have the right skills and experience to inflict such a change. On the contrary, high potential business in the developed countries have teams of people with common experiences and diverse but complimentary skills. In fact, the potential stakeholders look for carefully selected teams with experienced sales executives and executives in marketing, finance, sales and operations.

However in developing countries, these skills are equally needed and valuable, but is usually available in short supply. This is why the entrepreneurs here look for other skills localities have like the ability of seeing through the fog of politics and economics which prevails in crisis-prone developing countries.

Moreover, there is more trust in developing markets when compared to the developed markets, especially wherever there are well established arms-length transactions. This is the reason why you find many family owned and run businesses in developing countries when compared to the western or developed economies.

In other words, entrepreneurship in developing countries and developed countries are two different entities. While things are relatively easier for entrepreneurs in developed countries, those in developing countries have more challenges and consequently more fruits and satisfaction through their endeavors.

With access to finance being one of the differentiating criterion between the two, I move on to explain the concept of micro finance and the access to finances entrepreneurs in developing countries have.

9. Micro finance Role and Access to Finance

The poor in the rural or developing countries don't need subsidies. What they need much more is an access to credit. As they don't have any form of formal employment, they are 'non bankable' and can't get loans from banks.

They thus turn to local moneylenders for monetary help, who loan them money at exorbitant interest rates. This has in turn lead to the development of innovative institutional mechanisms which help enhance credit to the poor even without any form of formal mortgage.

Most of the time, poor people manage to slowly mobilize the necessary resources to develop the necessary enterprises and dwellings over time. However if they were provided with the necessary financial resources, it would have helped them leverage their initiative and in the process, accelerate the building of incomes, assets and their economic and financial security.

Lack of access to any credit

Unfortunately, conventional finance institutions don't always provide financial aid to low-income families and women. As they are usually denied access to any credit for any purpose, there's no point in discussing the level of interest rates and other financial terms. So the basic problem the poor people face is not unaffordable loan terms but instead, the lack of access to any credit.

This lack of access of credit to the poor is attributed to the difficulties which arise because of the mode of operation followed by financial institutions and the economic characteristics and monetary needs of low-income households.

For example, most commercial financial institutions require that people who borrow from them have a stable income source through which the principal and interest amount is paid back according to the stipulated terms. However most self-employed households here don't have a stable income.

Moreover, while the poor need numerous small loans, lenders prefer sanctioning few large loans as it helps minimize their administration costs. They also look for a clear title collateral which unfortunately most low-income households don't have. To top it all, bankers consider these low-income households more of a risk which only leads to high information monitoring operational costs.

However over the past decade, there have been many successful incidences where finance which was provided to small entrepreneurs at market rates with responsive market rates was repaid and used for increasing the poor people's income and assets.

This isn't actually surprising as the only other realistic option they had was borrowing from informal markets at a higher interest rate. With NGOs, grass root savings and community banks all around the world proving that micro enterprise loans are actually profitable to the borrowers and lenders, microfinance has now grown into one of the leading and most effective poverty reducing strategies.

Huge demand amidst the poor and women

Not only are microfinance institutions financially viable and self-sustaining to the communities they operate in, they also have the potential to attract more resources and expand services to the client. However though microfinance institutions are successful, only about 2% of the world's small entrepreneurs have access to financial services.

Moreover, though there is a huge demand for credit for the poor and women at market interest rates, it's only after the volume of financial transition of microfinance institutions reach a certain level do their financial operations become self-sustaining.

This means though microfinance has a promising institutional structure to offer credit to the poor, the scale problem has to be resolved to reach the many potential customers demanding access to market rate credit.

Accordingly, the question now is how microenterprises which provide short term capital finance to informal sector small businesses are not only sustained as an important part of the financial sector, but also how their financial services can be expanded based on effective principles, modalities and standards.

Reduce administrative costs

It's only if financial intermediaries providing services and generating domestic resources have the capacity to meet high performance standards will they grow successful. They also have to provide access to clients and achieve great repayments and work at operating and financial self-sufficiency so that they expand their client reach.

Microfinance institutions need to find means of reducing their administrative costs and broaden their resource base to achieve all this. It's possible to reduce costs by simplifying and decentralizing loan applications and its approval and collection processes. Even group loans wherein borrowers are responsible for most of the loan application process and where loan officers get to handle more clients and thus reduce costs.

By accessing capital markets, mobilizing savings and with effective institutional development support, microfinance institutions can easily and quickly broaden their resource base. Using a corporation which buys loans offered by microenterprise institutions using funds raised through bonds issued on the capital market provide a logical means of tapping the capital market.

Large scale lending operations also benefit through savings facilities. Studies have proven that the poor who work at the informal sector save money, which is why they value access to client-friendly savings service and access to credit. With savings mobilization, financial institutions are answerable to local shareholders.

This is why sufficient savings facilities is important for serving the demand for customers' financial services and to fulfill the leaders' financial sustainability. Microfinance institutions either provide savings services through deposits or make arrangements with other financial institutions to provide savings facilities which will flexibly tap small savings.

The important ingredients of successful savings mobilization are liquidity, location convenience, positive real rate of return and savings' security. Microfinance institutions become financial intermediaries once they get busy taking deposits to mobilize household savings. This leads to necessary prudential financial regulations which ensure the financial stability and solvency of the institution, and protects the depositors.

Encourage development of various institutions

However too many rules which do not take the microfinance institution and its operation into consideration hampers their viability. Regarding the size of small loans, microfinance institutions need a minimal capital requirement lower than the capital applicable to commercial banks.

Consequently, it's important that a more stringent capital adequacy rate which is the ratio between capital and risk assets should be maintained as microfinance institutions provide uncollateralized loans.

A legal and regulatory framework should be provided by the government to encourage the development of various institutions and let them work as recognized financial intermediaries which abide to simple supervisory and reporting requirements.

Relax usury laws

Microfinance institutions should not only be given the freedom of settling fees and interest rates to cover the interest revenues' operating and finance costs in a reasonable amount of time but usury laws should also be relaxed or repelled.

Government should also provide credit enhancement mechanisms or subsidies to lending institutions in their early stage of development to facilitate the transition process for reaching a sustainable operation level. Strengthened links with formal sector counterparts is one means of successfully operating microfinance institutions.

The comparative strengths of each sector determine a mutually beneficial partnership. Low transaction costs because of an adaptability and flexibility of operations provide microfinance institutions in informal sectors with a comparative advantage.

Microfinance institutions can handle credit assessment of the urban poor and absorb the loan processing transaction costs. Formal sector institutions can access broader resource-base and high leverage options using deposit mobilization.

Consequently, formal and informal sector finance institutions can form a joint venture where the formal sector institutions provide funds in equity form and the latter, provides funds through savings and loan facilities to the urban poor.

Another option or partnership could be one where formal sector lenders refinance all loans made by informal sector lenders. This helps the informal sector institutions tap additional resources and works as an incentive to exercise better financial management.

Serve as an intermediary

In some situations, microfinance can also serve as an intermediary between the borrower and formal financial sector and on-lend public sector guarantee backed funds. NGOs and similar businesses can offer commercial low-cost and risk funding to micro entrepreneurs through leveraged bank-NGO-client credit lines.

Under such situations, banks make one bulk loan to NGOs who packages the large loan into small loans at market rates and then recovers them. Though lots of research is going on about all this, some context specific research is required to identify the best model.

Some notable flaws in the system

One of the most successful microfinance models famous through the world is the Grameen bank which has successfully served the rural poor in Bangladesh without any physical collateral. They rely on group responsibility in replacing the collateral requirements. There are however a few weaknesses associated with the concept.

There is too much of external subsidy which is not replicable and Grameen bank does not work towards mobilizing the peoples' resources. The 50 weekly, equal instalments of the repayment scheme is not that practical as the poor don't have a stable job and thus have to migrate to other places looking for jobs.

Moreover, if the poor are agrarian during the lean seasons, they find it really difficult repaying the loan. This high repayment scheme creates pressure to the poor wherein they turn to money lenders for help.

Credit is not enough to alleviate poverty, and Grameen bank is based only on credit. Microfinance in fact takes time to get implemented and anything done in haste can lead to the wrong selection of beneficiaries and activities.

Moreover, most microfinance institutions find it difficult finding the skilled labor required for local level accounting. The dropout rate of their trained staff too is rather high. The option they can consider is automation, which is however not given much consideration as yet. Most microfinance institutions don't lend for agriculture too, so there hasn't been any testing for agriculture lending as yet.

Another example is the failures of many reputed microcredit agencies in the state of Andhra Pradesh in India. This failure is attributed to mismanagement, fraud and the overstretching of their limits at forcing borrowers to repay. With the agencies running afoul of the regulators, it lead to a full blown crisis.

All this shows that just like there are Central Banks and Regulators monitoring traditional and mainstream banks and financial institutions, monitoring and regulating the microcredit agencies should also be their responsibility.

Moreover, the government should ensure that the credit disbursement and repayment follows strict norms so that the greed of the agencies and the borrowers is contained and a new, balanced approach is followed.

How it may be possible to improve the system

Despite these drawbacks and flaws, microcredits have triggered a revolution in the poor and underprivileged in most Third World countries. Experts offer some suggestions to improve the system like broadening the base of borrowers to include artisans, cooperatives and medium scale enterprises, thus practicing the principle of group lending and in the process, fostering greater discipline and tighter procedural norms.

Other suggestions include improving the small entrepreneurs' skills so that they don't end up risking stagnation by doing the same skill base work they had taken the loans for.

One more point worth mentioning about microcredit is that once the borrowers achieve scale, their creditworthiness is enhanced so that they become more 'bankable' to financial institutions. This in turn qualifies them for long-term credit from traditional sources and set an example for other borrowers and potential borrowers to follow their fiscal discipline and repayment.

Forming Self Help Groups or SHGs so that each group member is given a seed capital, and the group funding, the SHGs are encouraged to rotate the seed capital among themselves and fund future growth through the revenues and accruals collected from past activities. These groups are inspired by the government or microcredit agencies to help themselves, and consequently the whole system.

There are many such groups located in India and other parts of Asia where they use seed capital and the initial funding to stand on their feet and grow independent and thus set an example for others to follow.

All this shows that microfinance institutions do indeed have a lot to contribute to alleviating poverty in third world and developing countries. The institutions help the poor build their financial discipline, and also educates the borrower about all the payment requirements to be met.

One aspect about microfinance which has caught my interest, and which I feel contributes in a great way at alleviating poverty is the concept of mobile banking. This is banking through your mobile phone, which has made finance so convenient and accessible to even to the poor today.

10. Mobile Banking Models and Poverty Assistance

THE BANK
IN YOUR POCKET

I've heard that women in many parts of developing countries like India and Philippines have a habit of hiding whatever money they save under the mattress or in some other similar places around the house.

The main reason they do this is because it's rather difficult, or perhaps impossible for them to say 'no' if and when a relative or friend comes to their home to 'borrow' money. Moreover, if they do end up lending them money, they are not assured if the amount will be returned, and it does not accrue interest.

Another problem is of course, because many of these women and other people in developing countries find it difficult accessing the few banks to open a savings account. Without any savings, these people find it rather difficult climbing out of poverty. This is where mobile technology steps in, and proves helpful at helping them gain a strong foothold by helping them save and even at times earn more money.

At present about 30% of households own mobile phones in developing countries, where cell phone coverage is widespread. While the advent of mobile society has led to convenience and a cultural change in US and Europe, affordable mobile phone access has led to a quantum leap in services like calling for medical help and starting a savings account in the poorest regions of the world, which the Americans and Europeans take for granted.

This is why Sach, the head of Earth Institute at Columbia University and the author of the 2005 book 'The End of Poverty' claims that the cell phone is the singular most transformative technology used and important for development. It is through mobile phones, and IT technology that the isolation and lack of access to education, markets, financial services and emergency health services and consequent poverty can come to an end.

The many benefits of mobile banking

There are many benefits associated with mobile banking, and one of them is its socio-economic impact. Developing countries like Kenya which have underdeveloped banking infrastructure, large population and a high poverty rate have experienced up to 80% increase in its financial inclusion.

Besides the improvement and significant changes in the agricultural production and global health of developing countries, the increased access to mobile technologies marks the starting point to something much bigger.

As most people in developing countries are not included in the country's banking system's infrastructure, if and when they do receive access to financial services, there is a marked improvement in their cash management. Moreover, this leads to a better infrastructure for business and the development of markets.

All this change in the infrastructure in developing nations will lead to a marked change in the way people live in the countries. And all it takes is a small technological innovation like the mobile phone to make such a huge impact to create a more developed economy in the countries.

These mobile phones now make it possible for the poor in the developing countries to make payments via their mobile phones. In fact, the use of cell phones in developing countries have tripled to more than 4 billion mobile subscriptions within a span of 5 years from 2005 to 2010.

The growth was fasted in Africa, where there was more than 400% growth in mobile use in the same time frame. The growth in mobile use signified more money, and a study conducted in the University of Michigan in 2006 showed that for every 10% increase in the cell phone penetration in a country, there was a 0.6% increase in the local economy.

All this was possible because of a phone call, with its far-reaching economic consequences. Moreover, the low cost of setting up of mobile towers and the rapidly dropping rates of handsets helped in expanding the cell phone coverage to even the poor and rural locations.

Moreover, new business models for selling phone services to the poor were set up like buying pre-paid phone services, and their being charged by the second instead of a minute, made cell phone usage more affordable to them.

It however was the development of banking services via cell phones which actually revolutionized the telecom business in poor countries. Through these monetary services, customers could digitally transfer their cash using their mobile phones instead of physically going to any bank to make the transfer. The system has many stores, and the poor can deposit and transfer their money to anyone of these stores.

This led to a marked increase in the country's GDP, which would have been half of what it was in the past decade if it wasn't for the mobile phone. As a result of mobile banking, more cash moves and stays in small villages, which in turn helps build up the local economy. With money being delivered locally, the locals needn't physically go to the nearest urban center just to collect cash.

Starting a business is also so much easier because of the mobile phone. In fact, the villages in developing countries now not only sell their locally available ware, but can now also sell 'city goods' like furniture and hair-straightening products for women, which was once unavailable in the village. All this was possible only because of the mobile phone and mobile banking.

Mobile phones not only released money flow in the developing countries, but also taught the people here terms like 'pin number', 'transfer' and 'account'. These terms were once technical foreign terms now provide for a nice transition at using financial banking services for the first time. People, especially women now realize its better using mobile phones and mobile banking instead of keeping all their money buried in the ground.

These people have a mobile phone, but not a bank account, making and proving that mobile phones are a direct conduit to more than half of the world's unbanked population. This proves that mobile or branchless banking can quickly reach the large number of the unbanked population.

Studies conducted on the outreach of 8 branchless banking providers around the world proved that these 8 providers had about 3.73 million active registered users where 37% of them were previously unbanked. Moreover, 5 of these providers could reach more clients who were previously unbanked than the largest microfinance institution in the same country!

Moreover, these 5 mobile banking providers grew quickly to overtake the largest MFI's customer base in a short span of 3 years. Of course, while the services offered by the MFIs, and the branchless banking providers may be different, both groups provide for financial services for clients who are willing to pay for the services.

Some success stories

Kenya's M-PESA is the biggest success story of mobile banking, and efficiently proves that branchless banking can reach the poor and unbanked people on a large scale by offering them access to valuable and important financial services. With this huge success story, it's not surprising that there's a lot of activity in this sub-Saharan Africa.

Besides Kenya, the countries with maximum active m-money users are India driven by the distribution of government payouts, Russia which uses advanced ATMs permitting both cash deposits and withdrawals and brazil where their bill payments at agents reaches practically every municipality.

At present, an increasing number of women in Indonesia use their mobile phones to sell payment and banking services to people who live in areas where these services are hard to come by. These women are called RUMA (Rekan Usaha Mikro Anda) agents, or rather 'Your Microbusiness Partner'.

These agents buy a base-model phone for $30 or a smartphone for $100 and pay only $7 a month for airtime to earn about $1.10 a day acting as agents for utility companies, local banks and telecom operators. They accept payments, deposits and provide withdrawals and the interesting thing is that they use only the cellular network for making payments and bank transactions, without any Wi-Fi.

As most of these agents were previously earning only about $2 a day mostly by running food stalls or similar kiosks, their job as RUMA agents helps lift them over the $2.50 per day income, which is above the World Bank's poverty line.

Not only do these agents give local families a safe and convenient place to transact, they also help people set goals and progress in life. The agents are not only conduits for their community's financial transactions and savings, they also use the system to save money for themselves.

The Grameena Foundation also operates similar microfinance services in Philippines where customers are encouraged and sometimes required to make small deposits on a weekly basis for their loan repayments.

As security of the transactions are important, customers can choose to have a PIN-biometric, smart card or chip based client authentication mechanism where the financial institution is the custodian of the money and daily transactions.

There may be limits set on the size of transactions to be done through agents while transactions like enrollment, withdrawal, deposit and balance inquiry are all done through the customers' SMS service.

Worldwide main barriers to mobile banking

It is true that the M-PESA scheme in Kenya was and is a great success. However despite all this enthusiasm, it's not easy replicating this success. All new providers in other countries have to be more innovative in their approach in introducing their products to the local market because of the following challenges the have to face:

Larger customer adoption- Though there are many m-money subscribers, only a small number of them are actually using the services. Most of the time, only a small percentage of the many registered branchless banking customers actually use the services. Lots has to be learnt about understanding customer demand, and developing and marketing their products effectively.

Changes in rules and regulations- Despite the huge m-money market, only a few countries actually have branchless banking or e-money rules. As branchless banking is still in an early stage, lots has to be learnt about enforcing the right level of regulation. There have been many legitimate concerns and questions raised about seemingly risky issues like conducting banking transactions in retail shops.

Better network of distributors and agents- It's possible to achieve large scale m-money operations only with a well-developed agent network. This network is required not only for providing important cash-in and cash-out services, but also for building trust for all first-time-users of formal financial services. Unfortunately as the business case for agents is rather small, there is a large agent dropout rate.

Business case-Obviously, branchless banks aim at making profits out of their business. Unfortunately, most of the time those who reap the maximum profits are indirect beneficiaries like MNOs who provide mobile money services have increased customer loyalty with its customers.

Thus branchless banking providers should consider offering various products to maximize their profits, and have not only customers, but other entities like companies paying salaries and governments who need to pay for social transfer payments into the system. For example, people in places like Kenya and Uganda can even use their mobile phones to pay at recharging stations to recharge LED lights.

It's clearly seen that mobile banking can indeed help eradicate poverty. There is a healthy increase in the adoption of the system and people are thus having increased control of their faith. It is this catalytic approach and work, and faith in their actions which leads to a real sense of empowerment among the people as they know they have a safe and confidential place to not only keep all their hard-earned money, but also easily access it as required.

11.Internet as an Innovation in Eradicating Poverty

It was during a speech at the UN on Saturday Sept. 26th 2015 that the Facebook CEO Mark Zuckerberg announced that he believed that the internet was the solution to eradicating poverty. He suggested creating a partnership between Facebook and the UN to work at eliminating poverty by 2030.

As part of the 17 Sustainable Development Goals committed to by leaders, improving access to resources would help eliminate world poverty. This means the poor and vulnerable will have equal rights to not only micro financing but also to appropriate new technology including internet access, financial services, natural resources and basic services. Zuckerberg's recent post states that by providing the masses with internet tools, knowledge and opportunities, the voiceless gain a voice and the powerful power.

Awareness

The internet thus helps create awareness as ignorance may be bliss, but is no longer excusable. With internet access, people around the world quickly and easily learn about the actual impact and extent of poverty exiting in today's world. People who once only heard about the prevailing worldwide poverty now learn astonishing and disturbing facts.

They learn about the tens of thousands of children who die because of poverty, that more than 3 billion people worldwide live on less than $2.50 a day and that millions of people die due to malaria even though it's easily preventable. Learning all about this makes the world more aware about the poverty situation and instigate many people to do something about this.

Similarly all this information and data available on the internet can be used to help the poor. With this data, we can now form a story about these people who have always been 'off-the-grid' or 'unbanked' as they say in the financial world.

As it was mentioned in micro financing, it's difficult for the poor to get a loan mainly because they don't have credit history. However things can be different if financial institutions started using this data to create a story about these 'thin-file' clients which traditional credit checks could not.

In addition to this, we can help the poor in millions of other ways. You can perhaps miss out on one restaurant visit a month so that you can use that money to support a child instead. Or perhaps you could buy an ox for a family overseas instead of buying a new car. Or if you have a habit of investing in the stock market, you could perhaps invest in the business dreams of an entrepreneur instead.

While these ideas may leave you with a small hole in your pocket and make your life a little less luxurious, they can make lots of difference to children dying of starvation. Whatever you donate lets these children live a long and productive life. The feeling of satisfaction you experience is well worth the sacrifices you make.

Advocacy

The internet will help advocate the cause of the poor as it can help organization communicate people's concerns to politicians. This is important as the government's support is very important and vital for eliminating poverty. The internet helps inform politicians that there will be consequences they have to bear if they do not live up to their promises, and if they do not do their bit at fighting against poverty.

Implementation of new ideas

It is a known fact that the internet is a form of springboard for lots of new ideas, including new ideas that can be used for fighting poverty. One such idea which developed through the internet is none other than micro financing and providing small loans to deserving poor entrepreneurs on a reasonable payout basis.

The internet has given birth to many programs which facilitate women employment opportunities and independence in the otherwise male dominated cultures and countries. The web now helps provide an opportunity to supporting entrepreneurship, creativity and independence in the poor people living in developing countries.

There are many people in these developing countries who have skills but don't know how or use the right avenues to use them to earn a living. There are mothers who cook great dishes who can work as chefs, men with green fingers who can turn a barren garden into a fertile one and even women who can aptly shuffle between their responsibilities and thus have the potential of leading any company! They need a means of using their skills to their benefit through these entrepreneurship avenues.

Helps harness the support of individuals

Not many people know that the power and support of individuals can help make a difference at combating poverty. The web helps congregate individual efforts to help create something which is much more powerful. This is in fact the driving force of the many sites and organizations which work at funding and providing support to the poor.

Moreover, it is now possible for people to gather together in communities with a much broader scope than it was possible before. In fact, the web now makes it possible to congregate individual efforts so that something more powerful is eventually produced. This is why you now find a marked increase in the number of Facebook groups, online communities and blogs which help people across the world come together to discuss their ideas and passion for eliminating poverty.

Provide feedback

The internet now makes it possible for everyone to actually practice actual democratic participation. It offers a platform for people to discuss the different social issues and consequently arrive at innovative solution to combat poverty.

People can now voice their suggestions to the government through this platform and even give their rating for all the government actions, policies and initiatives started for eradicating poverty. In other words, the internet now makes it possible for people to actually participate with the government to put in their share of efforts at eradicating poverty.

Provide education

Education is the main criterion for any person and country to move on and progress in life. However most developing countries don't offer any scope or means of their people studying more and moving on in life.

Most of the time it's because they don't have the funds to provide the necessary infrastructure to build an educational institutions. So to help them here, there are not only online tutors but many online schools and colleges offering courses which can be pursued from home without having to physically attend any college or institution.

These courses are made available to them at very reasonable prices and flexible classes are scheduled to help the students balance their work responsibilities and classes. While these rates may not seem much in developed countries for the developing countries poor, the amount seems to be as much as paying for full-time tuition in a private school.

All this proves that the internet is indeed a pivotal innovation at eradicating poverty. The internet not only facilitates effective communication, it offers various avenues for the poor to come out of their poverty and face a new facet of their lives. Of course, I must mention that it's not enough to just have internet connectivity it's equally important to create job opportunities and work. it's only if people are employed and have a means of earning money can poverty be eradicated.

12. Work force Creation in Eradication for Poverty

Poverty is the consequence of both underemployment and unemployment. It is only if the poor have a job can they find a means of supporting themselves and improving their well-being. This is why creating employment opportunities is vital at eradicating poverty and sustaining economic and social development especially amidst women and the youth.

An employed population leads to increased productivity and with it rapid economic growth. It is this economic growth which helps reduce and eventually eradicate poverty. Moreover, the ability of the poor at responding to these job demands in productive employment categories also plays a part in eradicating poverty.

It's not enough to just create jobs; the jobs created should be jobs the poor can work at, and not just any job. Remember, the poor don't have the funds and resources to pursue a normal education like others. So most of them are not that well educated.

If you ask me, I think that the perfect jobs to create for the poor are jobs related to agricultural and rural development. These jobs include jobs which require the use of labor-intensive agricultural technologies, development of both small and medium-sized enterprises and offering some avenues to promote micro projects in rural areas.

Then there are employment strategies which help promote and emphasize on self-employment amongst the masses, non-farm employment opportunities in rural areas and microfinance and credit to help generate employment and learn skills and the required training.

However these strategies generally work at meeting only the quantity of employment required whereas minimal emphasis is placed in the job's qualitative dimensions like dignity, freedom, security or equity.

So the focus should be on creating better and more productive jobs, especially those jobs which will provide to the employment needs of the large number of working poor. This will require making a substantial investment in labor-intensive industries, implementing changes in the structure of employment to higher productivity sectors and occupations and working at upgrading the job quality in the informal economy.

Besides all this, there should be some efforts at providing and teaching all these poor people with the required skills and assets wherein they will be able to take full advantage of any expansion in their employment potential.

Full employment scheme to narrow uneven distribution of unemployment

There is an uneven distribution of unemployment where the less-educated and disadvantaged faces the highest risk of unemployment when the economy drops. Similarly, the risks and rates of unemployment depends on the race too. Statistics have proven that amidst Hispanics, whites and African Americans, it is the African Americans who face highest risk of unemployment followed by Hispanics and lastly the whites.

To overcome all these hurdles, things will be better for the workers at the bottom of the income ladder to have an opportunity to work more hours. These are the people who are more than ready to put in extra hours on the job in a bid to earn more money. This is all achievable through a full employment policy which helps increase the opportunities and income of people at the bottom and consequently import their living standards.

If you take a look at the scenario at the end of the 1990s, you get a better understanding of the concept. This is when the unemployment was falling to a thirty year low. This is when the press had recorded incidences of suburban hotels and restaurants chartering buses to pick up their staff even from the inner cities, and drive them to their jobs in suburbs.

There were also incidents where employers provided their employees with day care facilities and even made arrangements to take care of aging parents so that their employees could come to work and work without any worries about their parents or children.

There were also some firms which sought out, and hired workers with disabilities. All this proves that in a tight labor market, firms will go to all means to recruit employees they may not have considered hiring at other times!

Moreover, full employment policy is desirable as it attacks the 'makers versus takers' line which conservatives tend to pull. So by not pursuing this policy, it means the employers are not putting their efforts of offering the masses with a work opportunity.

A full employment policy can be implement only with more government spending by investing in infrastructure, subsidizing pre-K education and retrofitting buildings to reduce greenhouse gas emissions.

It is also possible to lower the unemployment rates and eradicate poverty by reducing the trade deficit. So if it is possible to somehow increase exports but reduce imports by producing the required goods and services domestically, it not only improves the economy but also leads to more jobs. By completely eliminating the trade deficit and practicing balanced trade, it is easily possible to create millions of jobs.

Self-employment can help

While creating job opportunities does help eradicate poverty, the orthodox economy unluckily only recognizes wage-employment as jobs. There is no room or recognition for self-employment here, despite it being the quickest and easiest form of employment for the poor.

This means that instead of waiting for others to create a job for you, it's better and time for you to create your own job! This is a convenient option for those women who can't go to work but want to earn money and become independent. With self-employment, they can work out of their own homes.

This is exactly what our forefathers did years ago. They didn't wait for anyone to create jobs for them. They just created their own jobs and incomes in a routine manner. They were comparatively lucky as they had no economic theories to learn, and did not end up with a mindset that the only way they could earn money was to find a job in the job market. You just need to realize that if you don't find a job worthy of you, you need to march into the streets and create a job worthy of you.

So you can see, poverty can be eradicated. With the right job opportunities, there's no way poverty won't end up eradicated. Poverty has persisted all this while mainly because of the wrong mindsets which were created as poor people never realized, or got to realize their true potential. It is only when they once learn and explore their full potential, that the goal to eradicate poverty will grow into a thumping success.

13. Micro Entrepreneurship for Underserved

There is an acute shortage of underserved micro-entrepreneurs and low income people in countries with frontier or emerging markets. This is because as mentioned before, despite the fact that there is a high demand for these micro entrepreneurs, they are not covered by microfinance services.

Looking at this problem, many private, nonprofit, public and hybrid organizations work with the single aim of mentoring, training, educating and funding entrepreneurs. An example is the teaming up of Goldman Sachs with Berkshire Hathaway CEO Warren Buffet to launch a $500 million initiative to launch 10,000 small businesses and thus help the low-income entrepreneurs.

The New Jersey city based non-profit Rising Tide Capital is another group which reaches out to these struggling entrepreneurs of distressed communities. The organization was founded by Alex Forrester and Alfa Demmellash and offers one-on-one business training with a 10-week entrepreneurship course named the Community Business Academy.

Since its inception in 2004, the organization has worked and helped more than 250 people, mostly single mothers of Jersey City. The organization found out that there was a huge gap of services provided to low income entrepreneurs living in distressed inner cities.

This is because most of the established groups here like SCORE and US Small Business Development Centers concentrated on entrepreneurs who existed further along in their journey and not on the inner-city entrepreneurs. Forester and Alfa noticed that many micro-entrepreneurs like mothers offering day-care services didn't consider themselves to be small business owners and thus didn't use or turn to the existing educational and coaching services for help.

Any available resources was delivered to the far-off suburbs and office parks and not the inner-city population mainly because of lack of proper transportation. Not only did these groups find it difficult to find people to lend to, they were not easily accessible to the target population of underserved micro entrepreneurs. This is why Alfa wanted to start something different by being on the ground in the community and thus being easily accessible to those who needed their services.

Etsy

Then there's Etsy, which is an online marketplace providing an online platform for handmade, vintage and craft supply sellers to sell their ware to a global market. They have low barriers to entry for micro-businesses and give opportunities for micro entrepreneurs to earn some supplemental income and thus slowly move out of poverty.

Etsy had started their Craft Entrepreneurship Program which supports micro and solopreneurs by teaching business and e-commerce tools to people with artistic skills and thus provide them with the necessary support to start their own craft businesses.

Its five 2-hour classes include topics like becoming an Entrepreneur, Building and Marketing a Brand, Photography, Shop Management and Planning for Growth. In other words, the workshop teaches the micro entrepreneur all they should know to venture out into their new undertaking without any worries or apprehensions.

According to research, more than 115 million men and women in developing countries who receive micro-funding to start their business don't know much about the fundamentals of running a business. They just work at making goods and providing services so that they can make ends meet and take care of their families.

There are thus programs devised to provide a business foundation for these people. And as the internet is not reliable in developing countries and as most micro entrepreneurs have cell phones, the course is developed in such a way that all important information is accessed via the phone.

The course also have videos to illustrate the importance of running a small business. No matter which part of the world you may be, the fundamentals of running a business is to reach your customers, provide value and serve them well while generating revenue and making a profit. You also need to know how to manage your money and help your business grow.

This is all the consequence of a lack of financial institutions with sufficient products or capacities to serve this segment. Consequent weaknesses stem from a lack of cost-effective microfinance products, not much private investment in microfinance operations and insufficient microfinance methodologies managing them.

The best way to increase the availability of microfinance to the underserved in frontier markets is by creating a more developed microfinance industry while developing sound MFIs and promoting them. This can be done by promoting good corporate governance with sufficient lending techniques and new technologies proving that microfinance is available in countries with a less developed industry. Another MFI solution is to create, transform or strengthen the high performing MFIs so that they can grow and create a positive microfinance development impact on the regulatory framework and business environment.

Impact of Grameen bank

Microfinance options like the Grameen bank initiative in Bangladesh serves the low-income and poor population to help make them self-sufficient and come out of poverty. It was Muhammad Yunus who had founded the bank.

A Bangladeshi economist in Chittagong University by profession, it was while on a field trip to a poor village in 1974 that he and his students interviewed a woman who made bamboo stools. She used to borrow about 15p to buy the raw bamboo to make each stool and after repaying the middleman interest rates as high as 10% a week, she was left with hardly a penny profit margin. She would have earned a higher profit if she could borrow funds at better rates. Seeing this and deciding that something was wrong with the economics he taught, Yunus decided to take matters into his own hands.

He thus lent an amount equivalent to 17 to 42 basket-weavers from his own pocket and realized that it was possible to help them not only survive, but also create some personal initiative and enterprise needed to come out of poverty with this tiny amount. So while banks and the government were against this, he continued giving out 'micro-loans' and formed the Grameen Bank in 1983 based on the principles of trust and solidarity.

The bank today has 2,564 branches in Bangladesh serving 8.29 million borrowers from more than 81,000 villages. About 97% of the borrowers are women who have paid over 97% of the loans, and this recovery rate is much higher than any other banking system. The methods employed by the bank are applied in projects in about 58 countries including Norway, US, France and Canada. Mohammed Yunus was recognized for his Grameen Bank concept, and his contribution and efforts at helping the poor come out of poverty through a Nobel Prize in the year 2006.

So it's proven that if provided with the right support, even the underserved can come out of poverty. All they need is the right financial assistance and guidance and their hard work will help them earn sufficient money to sustain themselves.

Moreover, microfinance helps provide such low-income and underserved people with the access to savings, credits and other financial services they otherwise would never have had. It is with this financial assistance that the talented and hardworking people in developing countries finally have a means of becoming self-sufficient and even social entrepreneurs.

14.Social Entrepreneurship in Developed Countries

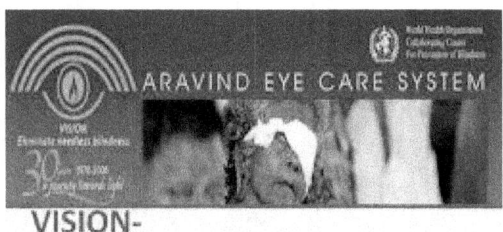

VISION-

ELIMINATE NEEDLESS BLINDNESS BY PROVIDING
QUALITY SERVICE IN REASONABLE PRICE TO ALL.

As mentioned earlier, social entrepreneurship describes businesses run with the aim of making money while solving social problems like high teen pregnancy rates, climate change or pollution or to help save endangered species. They are also referred to as not-for-profit organizations and is something every business should follow as business owners should find ways of surviving long-term without destroying itself.

With many entrepreneurs today making more money than thought was possible about 50 years ago, there is more money to go around to non-profit organizations. Entrepreneurs can thus spend more money on causes they are passionate about, like Bill Gates has through his The Giving Pledge cause.

This is an organization comprising of some of the world's richest people, mainly billionaires, who pledge more than half of their income in their lifetime or in their will. Examples of entrepreneurial members are Sara Blakely (Spanx creator and first self-made woman billionaire), Warren Buffet and Mark Zuckerberg.

It is the increased visibility of social causes via the internet which had prompted these billionaires and other successful worldwide entrepreneurs to make a significant global impact. Moreover there's actually no need of becoming an entrepreneur to pledge to global causes; there are sites like Kiva.org which lets anyone offer a micro-loan of $25 or more to entrepreneurs or business owners in developing countries.

Social entrepreneurship is not bound to only those in developing countries. It also exists in developed countries. Though these countries are developed, their social entrepreneurship can help the poorer nations in one way or the other.

The people in developing countries are constantly trying and fighting for their basic rights like improved healthcare, proper education and a means of earning money and eradicating poverty. So those in richer nations can do their bit by helping those in developing countries with their efforts. Developed countries can help them in many ways.

Help in healthcare

For one, they can help in the field of healthcare. Developed countries can help those in developing countries by sending their expert doctors to train the medical staff in developing countries. This social entrepreneurship can help improve the skills and knowledge of the doctors in developing countries.

Developed countries can also open free medical camps in some areas of poor countries to provide free medical advice to them all the time. They can also start health awareness campaigns to teach those in developing countries the consequences of an unhealthy lifestyle. They can also help with vaccination programmers in developing countries and thus help reduce infant mortality rate.

Then you have the Aravind Eye Care System which was established by Govindappa Venkataswamy in India in 1976 and has since then performed more than 4 million operations and has developed intra-ocular lens at a fraction of the import costs. SalaUno has replicated the Aravind model in Mexico and has carried out 133 cataract operations for free in a month for those who can't afford the treatment.

Help in education

Secondly, developed countries can offer help at educating the poorer nations. People in these countries can provide funds to open new schools and polytechnic institutions to help increase the country's literacy rate while providing vocational education.

Rich governments can also provide the students of poorer countries with scholarships providing them with an opportunity to study in the prestigious institutions providing scholarships. All this helps interest the poor to gain some higher education.

Promoting free trade

Thirdly, developed countries can help improve the poor countries' economy by promoting free trade. This helps them a lot as it reduces barriers to international trade like import quotas, export fee and tariff to help the poor come out of poverty.

Ok now that we know how social entrepreneurship in developed countries can help those in developing countries, here's the next question. Is this social entrepreneurship stoking the right type of required growth?

The question comes to mind because there are so many start-ups around where some may create fragmented efforts that eventually won't change much. Well, though there is a risk, these entrepreneurs can avoid this fragmentation through these three approaches which ensures even the smallest social enterprise has an outsized impact.

Scale of impact: It's a fact that most successful social enterprises reach only a fraction of the needy. For example, while Year Up is the biggest success story in US towards youth unemployment, though the organization mentors and trains disconnected youth through living-wage jobs, even after 10 years, the organization reaches only 2000 kids a year when there are 6.7 million young people out of school and work.

So organizations need to find a way to overcome this problem. They needn't grow their organizations but need to make the problems go away. Suggestions are introducing massive open online courses which provides education globally or the introduction of mobile apps which provide market and weather information to poor farmers worldwide or the use of national or global platforms to change social norms like designated driving and smoking cessation.

Not just organizations; lead collaborations are the need of the hour: The world needs leaders who can mix processes and relationships beyond the organization's four walls. For example, Bill Drayton, the founder and CEO of Ashoka who imparted the necessity of becoming a leader of teams of teams by sharing cancer therapy knowledge between labs across continents and oceans.

Then there's Kwabena Darko of Ghana who had managed to forge a collaboration between his startup Sinapi Aba, global NGO Opportunity International and various village and town-based trust groups to introduce the country's microfinance sector.

Giving power to voices. No matter if it is a far-flung or pint-sized idea, it can create a change if they unite and stem from someplace with deep authenticity. Entrepreneurs can help disadvantaged constituencies help themselves only if they teach them to give power to their voice.

The social entrepreneur needs to find ways for their constituents to influence and ownership over the solutions. Like Razia Jan, Afghanistan's Zabuli Education Center's founder provides Afghan girls with free education to empower them to speak up in their homes and communities.

Then there's MacArthur 'Genius' Award winner Mauricio Lim Miller of California who founded Family Independence Initiative, an initiative which helps low-income families first move towards economic mobility and then guide others.

So it's proven that not only the developing countries, but also developed countries need social entrepreneurs. Entrepreneurs in developed countries not only help their countries, but also other countries to help build a better and more peaceful and harmonious world.

Just like Robin Hood had once robbed from the rich to give to the poor to help the poor, the rich can use their money in such a way that it helps improve the economy of the world to make it a better place to live in. I feel that with the help of the ever-advancing technology and social platforms, all this is fun and easy to implement all over the world.

15.Micro finance in Developing Countries

What is the need of Microfinance ?

According to a 1995 World Bank estimate, in most developing countries the formal financial system reaches only the top 25% of the economically active population - the bottom 75% have no access to financial services apart from moneylenders .

We know that it was Dr. Mohammad Yunus who had started the Grameen Bank to provide capital to enterprising poor women without any collateral. Since its inception in 1977, the bank has served 8.04 million borrowers around the world with only a 2% default on the loans. Microfinance is not only accessible to poor women but also to the many poor unemployed entrepreneurs and farmers who are not bankable.

This was the start of the concept of micro financing, and since then, it has evolved astoundingly. "(Microcredit) is based on the premise that the poor have skills which remain unutilized or underutilized. It is definitely not the lack of skills which make poor people poor....charity is not the answer to poverty. It only helps poverty to continue. It creates dependency and takes away the individual's initiative to break through the wall of poverty. Unleashing of energy and creativity in each human being is the answer to poverty." (Muhammad Yunus, Expanding Microcredit Outreach to Reach the Millennium Development Goals, International Seminar on Attacking Poverty with Microcredit, Dhaka, Bangladesh, January, 2003).

Microfinance in developing countries provides poor people with an opportunity to start their own business and generate their own money to build up their wealth and slowly come out of poverty. In case of the extremely poor like destitute and the homeless, the microfinance institutions have special safety programs which first offer basic subsidence and then later graduate the members into their microfinance program by providing ordinary microcredits. The amount lent through microfinance is not much; seldom is it more than US$100.

Microfinance helps fight the multi-dimensional aspects of poverty by increasing a household's income. This in turn leads to increased food security, helps them build assets and offers an increased chance of the poor educating their children.

Microfinance also helps generate self-empowerment amidst the poor to help them make changes while increasing their income and become business owners. This in turn reduces their vulnerability while facing external shocks like weather, illness and more.

Microfinance was originally directed by the non-profit sector as commercial lenders need more forms of collateral to provide loans to microfinance institutions. However as the concept grew more popular and successful, the traditional banking industry has finally realized that these borrowers fit a new category of lenders called 'prebankable'.

With the industry realizing that those who cannot access traditional formal financial institutions still require various financial products, the mainstream financial industry now considers microcredit projects as a source of growth. Looking at the success of microcredit, the United Nations thus declared 2005 the International Year of Microcredit.

Emphasis on women

Most microcredit intuitions worldwide focus on providing microfinance to women in developing countries. Experience and observations have proved that women are comparatively a small credit risk who tend to repay their loans and work to benefit not only themselves, but their entire family.

Besides, providing microfinance to women is a means of helping them in a social economic way and to change the present conservative mindset and prove that women too can earn for the family. Moreover, women are mainly responsible for their children and their living in poor conditions leads to the physical and social underdevelopment of children.

With a World Bank report confirming that societies discriminate on the basis of gender go through slower economic growth, weaker governance, more poverty and lower living standards, with 70% of the world consisting of women and women having a higher unemployment rate in practically every country, women are in dire need of microfinance services. By providing them with microfinance, there is a huge impact on microfinance in developing countries which in turn benefits multiple generations.

Benefits of microfinance

There are various benefits of providing microfinance to developing countries.

- The main benefit is that it provides the poor with access to small size loans which banks do not provide to people with little or no assets. Micro financing believes the concept that even small amounts of credit proves helpful at eradicating poverty.

- Microfinance offers better repayment rates. Moreover, they target women borrowers as they are less likely to default on loans than men and as the loans empower women, they are a safer investment for the microfinances.

- Microfinance indirectly helps educate children. With money in their hands, families are less likely to pull out children from schools for economic reasons.

- Microfinance provides for better sustainability as even a small working capital loan of $100 to launch s small business in developing countries can help the benefactor and their family come out of poverty.

- Improved health is another benefit of microfinance as it provides improved access to clean water, better sanitation and health care.

- There is a reduction in domestic violence against women borrowers as they are regarded to be more valuable economic members of the family by generating an income through their micro-credit loans.

- Last but not least, microfinance provides new job and employment opportunities which will have an impact on the local economy. It gives these families which were once reeling in poverty a chance to earn money and plan a safe and stable future for their children.

It should be clearly understood that microfinance is not in any way a form of charity. Though it may have started out as philanthropy, it's a real business today. It works at extending the same rights and services to low-income and poor households which is available to everyone else. This thus provides them with protection from shocks and lets this part of the population have a part in the country's economy.

While some believe that microfinance may be guilty of over-promising and under-delivering to the masses, it still remains to be an effective development tool. As long as the rich world redoubles its efforts to extend additional resources to microfinance and find ways to bring successful programs to scale, microfinance will definitely flourish and help eradicate poverty.

One thing which still lacks in most microfinance initiatives is the provision of a mix of products meant for the very poor like loans with graduated interest rates and more flexible savings products. Studies have also proven that delivering other services like health information, business training and basic literacy with microfinance works better at reducing poverty. It helps create positive synergies which may break the cycle of impoverishment and an effective delivery mechanism for social services.

One should however remember that not everyone is a born entrepreneur, and thus are not suited for microfinance. While some people may excel in their business ventures and successfully lift their families out of poverty, many borrowers just use the borrowed money to improve their short term chances of survival.

These people may fail in their endeavors, risk falling into indebtedness and facing the wrath of the borrowing group to thus shame their families. This is why microfinance institutions targeting the very poor should take steps to minimize the number of borrowers who fall in this group.

This can be achieved by screening business concepts and providing help instead of loans to those who cannot produce and follow a repayment plan. Moreover, a segment of the poorest populations, like the old, displaced by war and the infirmed may just not be suitable microfinance clients. Just like all the fingers on your hand are not alike, people too differ. Only those born to be entrepreneurs can become one with the right motivation, help and guidance.

16. Access to Funds and Mobile Banking

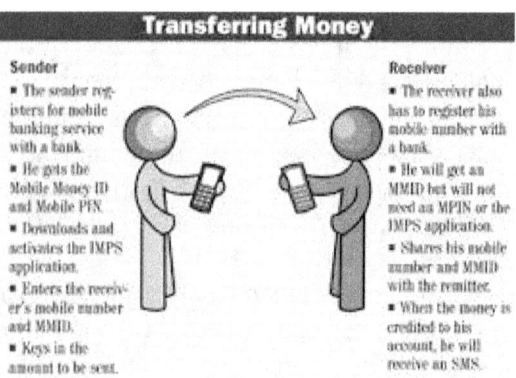

People living in the modern world have their own savings accounts which they use to save their money as part of financial management so that they have money to back on in the future. However those living in developing countries are not as lucky as they unfortunately don't have access to basic banking services and thus a savings account.

In fact, more than 77% of the people here don't have a savings account as there's not much incentive for banks to invest in such areas. So though the poor have money to save as they don't have bank accounts, they can't invest their own money and don't have access to credit. This not only prevents them from getting out of poverty and having money to rely on during a disaster, but also forces them to save money using insecure means.

This is how and why the concept of providing access to funds for the people in developing countries through mobile banking was started. This is made possible as technology is so viable and there is a large influx of mobile phones in developing countries.

While about 89 cell phones account for 100 people in developing countries, there are still thousands of impoverished people without any phones. However as the amount of people who do have a phone is hopeful, the concept of mobile banking for the poor could be implemented, and is a success.

The concept

The concept of access to funds through mobile banking is easy to understand. The person just has to transfer money from an employer, family member or even a hospital paying someone bus fair to access important medical procedures using mobile phone text.

The money either goes into a savings account or is exchanged for cash on going to a local authorized agent who is anyone from the local grocer or an automated kiosk the mobile banking company had set up. Even if there is no access to kiosks, the thought that this concept lets people save money is indeed beneficial.

Benefits of mobile banking to those in developing countries

The main benefit is that it is completely free of cost so people using it can avoid paying expensive banking transaction costs.

The second benefit is that mobile banking lets the mobile banking companies collect data to use to create credit scores for the customers who have little or no ability at building their credit or accessing any form of credit.

Added security is another benefit. People in the developing country had to depend on middle men to transfer money from one person to another who in the process, usually mishandled the money. Or they had to personally travel to deliver the money to a third person. All this has stopped, and is prevented by transferring money through mobile banking, which in turn helps save time and is much safer as the money directly reaches the recipient.

A very important benefit is that even the illiterate can make use of mobile banking. As long as they know how to use their cell phones, and know how to read numbers, they can comfortably and confidently depend on mobile banking for all their monetary needs.

Importance of mobile banking

With mobile banking, people in developing money can now save money. Their governments seldom provide safety net services, health care and other similar services to help keep them afloat if any financial disaster occurs.

However now with their own savings, the chances of their falling into poverty if an unforeseen life emergency occurs is reduced. Moreover, mobile banking companies give them incentives to save money and constantly send them reminders through text notification about when they need to save money.

Instead of nonprofits handing out food and clothes to locals, if the locals learn how to save money, they can use their saved money to buy whatever they require. Once they start buying things for themselves, they sense a feeling of achievement and pride. They learn to, and are adept at making good decisions about spending their money and finally have control on their own lives.

A typical example of successful mobile banking-M-Pesa

M-Pesa is a mobile banking company developed by telecom giants Vodafone and Safaricom with the blessings of Central Bank of Kenya in Kenya which lets Kenyans store and transfer their money using only a cell phone and SMS messages.

About 62% of the adult population in Kenya has an account with M-Pesa. It has not only helped account holders save money, but also let far away family members send them money during financial hardship so that they could continue maintaining their regular lifestyle and set to keep their children in school.

M-Pesa also lets its customers sign up for loans and interest accruing savings accounts on their phones. Their kiosks distribute actual cash which proves beneficial for those near them. While it is a bit difficult letting people in extreme rural areas gain access to the kiosks, it's much easier and cheaper than their building entire banks as kiosks are small and easy to maintain.

Bill Gates states that digital banking solutions like M-Pesa is a technology which will revolutionize the lives of poor in the near future. He wrote in his annual letter that "In the next 15 years, digital banking will give the poor more control over their assets and help them transform their lives. By 2030, 2 billion people who don't have a bank account today will be storing money and making payments with their phones. And by then, mobile money providers will be offering the full range of financial services, from interest-bearing savings accounts to credit to insurance."

While many were skeptical about this plan, and wondered if it can really transform the lives of all those people living on only a few dollars a day, Kenya has proven that mobile money has a dramatic influence in a country's economy.

While less than 30% of the adults in the country had access to formal financial services in 2006, the number has reached more than 65% since the implementation of M-Pesa. This has made M-Pesa the most successful mobile money service in the developing world. The service had processed more than $20 billion in transactions in 2014, which is more than 40% of the nation's GDP.

Not the same story everywhere

However replicating the success of M-Pesa in other developing countries was not so simple. Mobile money services were pushed for expansion in countries like Brazil, Nigeria and India between 2010 and 2013 but the pace of adoption was dismaying. While there were about 200 of these experiments across the world, only 4-5 were successful states Michael Joseph, director of mobile commerce at Vodafone.

One main reason for M-Pesa's rapid success was that it was offered by Safaricom, the nation's dominant mobile carrier. People thus easily trusted them with their money and growing was easy with the lack of competition and fragmentation.

Even Kenya's institutional dysfunction proved advantageous where its underdeveloped banking industry, unstable government and unreliable roads made M-Pesa an appealing option. According to Peter Wennemacher, the mobile baking analyst with Forrester Research, it were these same reasons for success in Kenya for mobile banking not succeeding in the more developed and tightly regulated markets.

Moreover, criminals used M-Pesa to move illicit proceeds in Kenya where laundering dirty money was made as easy as sending text messages. Most countries are however reluctant to let illegal transfers like that develop.

In countries like India which already has a robust banking sector, that banks are inclined to protect their existing revenue streams and thus do not give much motivation to innovate. Moreover, there are lots of regulatory pressures some tech innovators don't face.

Things have changed

However of late, mobile money has found its stride and learnt from its mistakes after the M-Pesa boom. Mobile banking now has well-established markets with various competitors across Asia, Africa and Latin America.

In fact, research from the Groupe Speciale Mobile Association, which is funded by the Gates Foundation, proves that the number of mobile money services across the globe has increased from just 64 in 2010 to 255 at the end of 2014.

In fact, mobile money services has more than tripled in size over the last two years in Bangladesh since the launch of state-sanctioned mobile money services in 2010. Mobile banking is also safer, faster and less expensive than traditional banking in Philippines.

So now it boils down to one question- will mobile banking actually help at eradicating poverty? Well, Claudia McKay of Consultative Group to Assist the Poor thinks that, "There is some evidence that the basic deposit, withdraw and send functions help poor people to have more choices, more convenience, more privacy and more security in their financial live."

She also said that it's just that people thought it was a magic service that would pull them out of poverty. However saying mobile money would actually help pull people out of poverty would be going too far.

So basically, mobile banking will help address some important issues including corruption as dealing with cash in economies with lots of corruption ends up with half of the wages gone before you receive the money. This is avoided with the government using mobile to pay wages.

Additional services can help

Experts also believe that in the long run, layering additional services over the basic mobile financial platform will have a significant impact on poverty. For example, M-Pesa in Kenya now partners with banks and companies to offer various services and financial products to its members. These services will slowly offer innovative offerings like special savings or credit plans related to farming and education.

An example is M-Shwari in Kenya where customers not only earn interest on their money, but on developing good credit, they can also access loans to help make big purchases or start a business. M-KOPA is another company in Kenya offering cheap solar panels with M-Pesa at the heart of the business. These solar panels are a boon to the 35 million people in Kenya who used to depend on kerosene lamps for light and borrowed car battery power to charge their cell phones.

M-Kopa sells their products for a small down-payment of $30 and the rest is sold in instalment over the year. Each solar panel has a SIM card connected to a Safaricom cell powered network so that users can pay their bills using M-Pesa. Though they can't draw power if they miss payment, they can switch back when finances stabilize.

And as Gates told the Verge, it's an economical idea of banking where the very poorest bank not through branches or ATMs, but with the cellphone. He also said that with the strong demand for banking amidst the poor, and as the poor can be a profitable customer base, entrepreneurs in developing countries are now doing exciting work.

So no matter which part of the world you lived in, there is no worry if traditional banks can't or won't serve the large portion of the population. This is when and how the technology lying in our pockets will help fill the gap.

17. Identifying the Beneficiary without disclosure in society

The problem however is if the technology lying in our pockets, as mentioned in the previous chapter, actually does reach the poor or beneficiaries? Now you wonder how it is possible to distinguish poor clients and how microfinance actually targets the poor. What are the best approaches to target the poor? NGOs, donor, organizations like CGAP and practitioners have been tackling the matter and have managed to come up with some clear answers.

The first thing that everyone agrees upon is that microfinance is not a magic potion which automatically gives better living conditions for the poor. In some cases, it has in fact deteriorated situations and debt equity ratio of the very poor instead of improving their lives. This is why it's better and important to implement careful targeting measurements.

Different methods of poverty measurements have been used where the most common is based on income or consumption levels. Here, a person is considered poor if his/her income or consumption is below a certain minimum level or poverty line which can vary in time with the geographical contexts, social norms and values.

According to the Micro Credit Summit, the poorest are those who belong to the lower 50% of people living under a country's nationally defined poverty-line. The World Bank declares that the poor are those with a level of consumption of $2 per day and the poorest, a level of consumption of $1 a day. Other dimensions also define poverty like education, health, vulnerability, and social exclusion, access to social capital and access to infrastructure.

It's not easy measuring poverty as aspects like health, leadership, life, women's roles and empowerment are difficult to quantify. It's also expensive coming to precise poverty measurements.

There is no general agreement that microfinance should target the poor to have a real impact on poverty. Some argue it's important to have a wider permanent geographical impact using quality financial products delivered by effective micro-finance institutions.

How microfinance fails to reach the poor

To understand how and why microfinance doesn't reach the poor, you need to borrow the metaphor of a leaking pipeline which illustrates how some households miss the pipeline of participation. No matter how well planned you may think the pipeline is, there will always be some unexpected or unforeseen leakages wherein everyone down the line receive less water than expected or needed.

- The first is that the poorest may not receive information about upcoming awareness meetings and thus don't know about the groups to be initiated. Though relevant information may spread through informal channels and actual meetings, there is a chance that the poorest are excluded from these information networks as well.

- Secondly, only some of those who receive the information may actually be interested in the idea. Some may think that they do not require the group's services or they may think that they may not find a group which accepts them at this stage.

- Thirdly, some of the interested may get left out of the group formation as it occurs voluntarily. Villagers have to form groups with others they trust from the village. In such cases, assort tie matching may take place where the riskier borrowers join to form groups as per the traditional theory of information symmetry (Ghatak and Guinnane). The outreach may get affected with poverty status correlated with risk aversion as only a few groups are formed in each village. Consequently, as poorer households are considered less advantageous to groups they may find it difficult finding one.

- The fourth reason is that once groups are formed, they are usually formed with some attrition. Sometimes the poorest may not find useful groups to join or in some other cases, or other members may pressurize them to leave the group.

- The fifth reason is that even if the poorest do stay in the group, they may not use all the group services. They may either not have the non-credit resources required to make use of loans or as they may have too volatile an income, they risk an involuntary default wherein they focus on smoothing income instead.

Identifying the poor

Microfinance companies have developed various strategies to identify the poor which includes ways of identifying and attracting the poor and ways of excluding and discouraging the non-poor. For its effective targeting, all these components have to be included using agent-related factors like client's needs, constraints and type of MFI, impact, microfinance outreach like how many people are reached, how poor the clients are, where they live and the sectors they are engaged in and contextual factors like infrastructure and regulatory framework.

Target measurement

Lots of research has been conducted by organizations like CGAP to establish efficient cost-conscious methods of measuring how well micro-finance programs reach the poor. The results are however disappointing as it does not reach any tangible conclusions.

The CASHPOR Housing Index is used by Grameen Bank networks in the Asia-Pacific region which is highly related to the house quality and status. Three dimensions are considered here viz. the roof material, size of house and its physical condition or building materials.

The poor and less poor are ranked in geographical and social context where the poorest are those living in houses built using mud bricks, small windows, low quality thatch roofing and a generic state of disrepair.

The Participatory Rural Assessment (PRA) and Participatory Wealth Ranking (PWR) lets communities rank themselves based on their perceptions of poverty. Detailed discussions are held in communities to define poverty and rank the community based on participatory rural mapping and wealth ranking. An attractive aspect of this approach is that it lets people define their own concepts of poverty and wealth.

Geographical distribution of poverty

The geographical concentration of poor households help micro-finance practitioners target the poor using locations as proxy while taking into consideration variables like quality of public services, rates of illiteracy, infant mortality and life expectancies. There however is a limitation that it may include non-poor households.

Vocation

The nature of activity also helps determine income levels, along by identifying the location of enterprise.

Small loans

Loan size is sometimes used as a proxy to check the outreach in microfinance. Some programs work at selecting the poorest area in a region as its operational area based on the theory that small loans with high transaction cost in terms of time spent entering the program and participating in long meetings would not deter everyone but the very poorest from joining. In some cases, like agricultural loans, the loans are larger than average while the clients may be poorer.

House-to-house interviews

Household or client interviews and surveys were conducted to determine the family's poverty where evaluators met people in their homes, observed the household conditions and asked questions about family members, expenses, food consumption and sources of income. However the limitation here is the inaccuracy of income and expenditure surveys.

Other methods

Sri Lanka's Ruhunu UNESCO completes cards for each beneficiary family using information collected through surveys of the family's circumstances and poverty level which included factors like housing quality, health, meals per day, monthly income, number of school-going children and electricity.

With the help of these tips and approaches, it will be easy and possible to identify the beneficiary without any social disclosure. Once the beneficiaries are identified, the next step involves in developing their mind map to eradicating poverty.

18. Developing their Mind Map

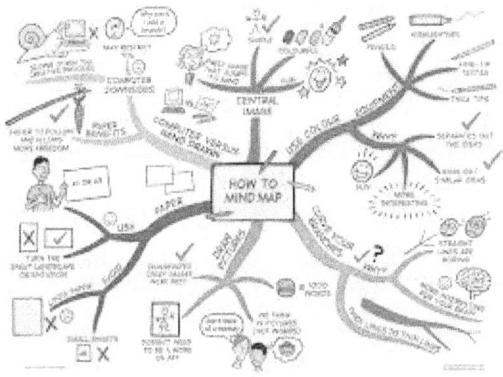

So now the next question which obviously jumps to your mind is what exactly mind mapping is. Well, a mind map is actually a visualization of your thoughts. When you have an idea, like eradicating poverty here, you find that everything just seems to radiate from your head at one time. You feel like it's a supernova, a 360 degree explosion, which you find difficult capturing in your mind. You also find it difficult organizing your thoughts, and communicating it to other people.

This is when you need the help of a mind map to not just relate your thoughts to all the poor people, but relate them in an interactive manner so that their creativity is triggered. Mind maps can be considered to be informative, colorful, memorable and highly organized diagrams which help 'map out' your idea.

The concept of mind mapping was developed by Tony Buzzan, who had spent a life's work working at a powerful technique to capture ideas, thoughts and inspirations. He argues that readers traditionally scan information from left to right and from the top to bottom.

However the brain's natural tendency is to scan the entire page in a non-linear fashion. His concept has grown so popular worldwide today that it has gained millions of fans worldwide and helps Buzzan earn over 100 million pounds annually.

The main benefit of mind mapping is that it uses both the left and right brain-thinking tools which helps enhance your thinking's clarity, structure and organization. It is a thinking tool which uses all the significant and potent ways of thinking into its structure.

How to make a mind map

With the mind working on various thoughts and directions at the same time, you need to start with an image in the center of a blank sheet of paper. Then draw connectors from it, branching out all over the page.

As mentioned earlier, you need to use both sides of your brain to develop your idea. The right side is needed for dimensions, images and colors while the left part is needed for words, logic, analysis and numbers. It's your job to capture all these points on a single page in an associated manner, and the resulting diagram you get is a mind map.

In other words, you need to make the most use of your brain as most people don't. Most people think that color, daydreaming and imagination are all wrong and childish actions. You think that using your color and being playful is nonsense when it's not. Mind mapping teaches you to not only completely utilize your brain but also to remove all the blindness people have been brought up with.

Mind mapping and poverty eradication

So in the case of using mind mapping for poverty eradication, you slowly but easily and naturally help the poor to make maximum use of their creative abilities to reap maximum profits. You teach them that it's only if you completely use their brains will they get the best ideas to eradicate poverty. This is why even business schools today include mind mapping as part of their teaching curriculum.

Once you teach them to use mind maps on an everyday basis, they will slowly but surely find that their lives become more productive, fulfilled and successful on all levels. As there are no limits to the number of thoughts, ideas and connections anyone can make with mind mapping, they learn that there are no limitations to the number of ways mind maps can help them.

Things needed for mind mapping

With mind mapping being so easy and natural to do, you need to show them how to make a map. This is easy to do as only a few ingredients are necessary for effective mind mapping. They are your brain and imagination, of course, and some blank, unlined paper and colored pens and pencils.

Now you have to start at the center of a blank page which is turned sideways. The reason you start from the center is this is how and where you give your brain freedom to spread itself in all directions, and to express itself much more freely and naturally. So this is where your main idea or reason for the map, which in this case is poverty eradication.

You need to start with an image or picture as your central idea. You start with an image as an image is always worth a thousand words, and helps you with your imagination. Moreover, central images are more interesting, give you more focus and concentration and also gives your brain a buzz.

It's important that you use colors while mind mapping as colors are exciting to your brain as images. Moreover, color adds vibrancy and life to your mind map which in the process adds energy to your creativity.

Now you need to connect all your main branches to the central image and connect all the second and third level branches to the first and second levels. This is necessary as your brain works based on association and likes linking two or three things together. Moreover, once you connect all the branches, you make understanding and remembering the mind map much easier.

It is in these branches which you implant the various ideas you have to eradicate poverty like microfinance, creating employment for youth, giving them the required training to work and women empowerment.

It's better if all the branches in your mind map are curved and not straight lined as just having straight lines in your map is boring to your brain.

While the main ideas are the branches in a mind map, smaller and less important topics associated to poverty eradication are represented as 'twigs' of the relevant branch. For example, the twigs for microfinance may be the many institutions associated with microfinance or how to apply for microfinance or perhaps how women empowerment can be achieved like self-sufficiency, savings and jobs.

Mind maps work better if you use one keyword per line. By using one keyword per line, you automatically give your mind map more power and flexibility.

Make it a point to use images throughout the mind map. This is important as like the central image, these images too are worth a thousand words. So if you look at it this way, having 15 pictures on the mind map is equivalent to having 15,000 words of notes on the map!

Moreover, it has been proven in 1970s Scientific American magazine that people have a recognition accuracy of images between 85-95%. People find it easier remembering and associating images as they use lots of cortical skills, especially imagination. Moreover, images are more evocative than words and can trigger lots of association which in turn enhances memory and creative thinking.

Consequently, the poor associate better with colors and images than words, so using images and colors in the mind map makes it easier for them to understand the concept. They can understand and remember the idea better and this facilitates for better and more efficient implementation of your ideas.

All the branches and images of the map will eventually form a connected nodal structure which helps the poor understand your poverty eradication idea much better. Now that you know the importance and need of mind mapping in your endeavor to eradicate poverty, the next thing on my agenda is to identify the interested and potential candidates.

19. Identify the Interest and Develop Custom Solutions

The best way to get about overcoming poverty is by developing custom solutions to help the poor earn money and become self-sufficient. The poor are in poverty not because they want to, but because they have no alternative. There are various reasons that keep the poor in poverty; it's only by recognizing these reasons can you help them.

A lack of basic skills is one such factor. Most of the people living below the poverty line find it difficult reading, writing, doing basic math and lack English proficiency, which are required for employment.

Moreover, the lack of these skills lead to a lack of computer literacy and difficulty in learning new skills as they can't read and understand high level instructions and manuals. All this makes it practically impossible to keep even menial, low-pay jobs.

Another factor is a lack of employment skills. At the most, the poor may have a strong back and ability to sweep a floor and do some gardening. They don't have any more skills, and in addition to this, don't have other generalized skills needed while working like getting up on time to maintain punctuality, treating colleagues reasonably and having a reliable mode of transportation.

Unfortunately, while one or a combination of these two can label a family 'working poor', they will not earn enough to come out of poverty. Moreover, as they work at low-wages they won't have health insurance and are ineligible for Medicaid.

Substance abuse makes things worse

While many people with physical disabilities can thrive in the society taking their disabilities into stride, there are other severely disabled people who cannot work and depend on public assistance. Those with intellectual difficulties and function at the level of young children are also dependent on their adults or public for assistance. While those placed in caring group homes live a high quality life, life is however grim for those who have no support and outside resources.

Those dependent on drugs or alcohol can lead to poverty as the purchase of drugs and alcohol drains resources. Moreover, drug and alcohol dependent people are unlikely to show up for a job that pays well or maintain relationships or stay out of trouble.

To make problems worse, substance abusers generally lose their moral compass and do anything to get the drug they require. They also grow offensive or violent when drunk or high and all this leads to the fairly quick breakdown of all the networks they might have had. Family and friends can tolerate this to a certain level and one day, they no longer have sober connections to give them a place to sleep.

Hard bad luck can affect anyone. All it takes is a single disaster like an unexpected medical catastrophe of cancer or an accident, a lost job, a divorce or losses to destroy a person's financial structure. Such people find themselves in a downward spiral ending in poverty and isolation.

Culture of poverty

Then there is the culture of poverty consisting of families which have been poor for generations. While it's not possible to estimate exactly how many are part of the culture, but it does exist. These people have been raised in poverty and are not taught the values, habits and attitudes needed to be self-sufficient in life mainly because their parents weren't taught them too.

This ends in a cycle of lack of interest and respect for education, consequent lack of skills and credentials and lack of belief that life can be different for them or their children. While this view is broken most of the time, it happens only after a change in world view and support for change.

These are the main problems faced by people, and the reason for their poverty. Once these problems are identified, it seems much easier developing customized solutions to help eradicate poverty.

Tips for customizing solutions

- Keep their needs in mind. For example, most of the people in poverty ridden countries can't speak or read English. In such cases, an ESOL class is the best place to start with perhaps some native language job training. Then there are people who have to resolve other things like domestic abuse, homelessness, substance abuse, mental illness or parental needs before seeking employment or other opportunities.

  Some may need citizenship or a green card or an understanding of basic economics like saving or the future and how to avoid debt. It's only after resolving or at least addressing such problems will people be able to move on in life. This is why your solution should involve reasonable and appropriate opportunities for the intended people.

- Keep the nature of the community in mind. Offer employment training in places where participants can get jobs on completing the program or course. There's no point training them for a dying industry or one with lots of job-seekers as it will not help them out of poverty.

- Try to enlist people you think will benefit in the planning and customization process. They are more likely to embrace the opportunity, and gain from it if you involve them in the planning process.

- Even the poor are respected people and should be respected regardless of their education, income or other factors. Once you show respect and approach them as people with rich experiences and knowledge, they start seeing themselves as worthy people capable of taking control of their lives.

- Set opportunities with clear and reachable goals which participants can see and experience this way they make better progress; and the more progress they see, the better they feel about themselves and the more clearly they believe that the can come out of poverty.

- Give them the emotional and psychological support to change their way of thinking as the poor don't usually think that their lives can be any different. They don't believe they can take action and think they can only be acted upon. Once they believe they can have an effect on their lives, there is a better chance of their taking steps towards change.

- Work at providing them with the daily survival support like paid leave and paid sick days. The main reason for failure of most welfare-to-work and other similar programs is that the required physical and logistical support like a child care or at least paid leave to take care of their sick child and rent subsidies is cut off as soon as participants get a job. It's imperative that support remains in place till an alternative is found or till a participant earns enough to be self-sufficient.

- Give them time to change as while some only need an opportunity to change their lives, others need to change their attitudes and world view before changing their lives. This may take time as it usually enlists throwing away a lifelong thinking.

- Ensure each individual has access to clean water, food, housing, electricity and healthcare. As governments should preferably move on to other projects only after ensuring this, this proves to be the hardest step to implement.

- Work at redistributing wealth as its imperative at eradicating poverty. Instead of the rich getting richer and poor getting poorer, tax should be tailored to a person's financial bracket to ensure upward social mobility.

- Creating self-sufficient economies by reducing dependence on external financial aid, oil and imports helps with poverty eradication. Steps to be taken include investing in local infrastructure, schools and transport and launch of new industries and businesses help keep the ball of development rolling.

- Raising minimum wages creates a huge boost at eradicating poverty. The minimum wages set in the 1960s was sufficient to help a family of three out of poverty, but not today. Inflating wages will thus help lift millions out of poverty.

- Supporting pay equality amidst men and women also helps cut poverty for working women and their families. Pay equality also helps add to the nation's gross domestic product.

So all this shows that there is nothing inevitable about poverty and that it's not difficult to not reduce it. There may be lots of hurdles in the path, it's your job to realize the poor's interests and problems, and accordingly customize a solution to help get them out of poverty. As the poor are unskilled and usually illiterate, after customizing your plan, you need to train them to be ready to be a part of, and face the work force.

20. Put them to Training and Prepare for Work force Inclusion

While the world's youth population larger than ever before now, one in eight are unemployed and over a quarter are trained only in jobs which keep them on or under the poverty line. Investing in their skills is a smart move for all countries working at boosting their economy.

Skills development is important for reducing poverty and enhancing employability. It helps the working poor and vulnerable groups like people with disabilities, rural communities, disadvantaged youths and women who face difficulties and discrimination in accessing good quality training necessary for better work.

On an average, each dollar spent on a person's education yields about $10 to $15 in economic growth across the person's working lifetime. So it's important that the funding for fixing this skill deficit is increased.

Not only do governments and donors have to find the money and energy to help the youth acquire their skills, the private skill which benefits from a skilled workforce also has to increase its financial support.

Accordingly, the International Labor Organization now concentrates on extending training to rural communities, upgrading informal apprenticeship systems and helping at improving skill development and employability to meet the special needs of Africa.

Training and counselling

Their Rural Economic Empowerment (TREE) Programme starts with institutional arrangements and planning with organizations at national and local levels. This program helps identify the potential community level economic opportunities and uses local public and private training providers to deliver community based training programs.

The training the poor should be given can be divided into various types based on their individual capabilities and training needs.

Pre-employment skills training is best for those who haven't worked before and have not developed any skills, habits or attitudes needed for successful employment. It may include a training program including job-finding skills like how to dress, self-presentation, resume writing and how to respond to questions during a job interview.

The program may also include tips at maintaining work relationships to get along with coworkers and supervisors and conflict resolution, learning about basic employment responsibilities like reaching work on time, finding suitable transportation, informing employers when sick or during emergencies, knowing when they can or cannot miss work and general employment related information like minimum wages, working of payrolls, safety concerns, workers and employers' rights and payroll taxes and benefits.

Career counseling is necessary for successful employment opportunities. It involves helping the poor understand what their skills are, what they enjoy, what training they require to join a particular job and the available job opportunities help in both creating and choosing a program or direction. With the right counselling, the poor know how to choose a lifelong career than one job at a time where they stay with the job and are more likely to undergo more training or education and get promotions.

Employment training benefits those who have a job history or understand the world of work but have no specific skills. Training here includes specific job training in a trade or career field like auto mechanics, typing/word processing, call center jobs, certified nurse's aide training and transferable skills like computer literacy and business management.

Protected workshops

Protected workshops provide employment in sheltered environment for people suffering from severe disabilities or developmental problems. With this employment, they start feeling like productive members of society wherein they earn cash and are self-sufficient to take care of their personal needs.

The poor who are ready to work can benefit through jobs from government or funded programs like job banks, state employment agencies and job development and employers who are committed at hiring a fixed number of poor people and provide them with on-the-job training.

These poor people can also partake of internships, get help like loans, business courses and technical support and work with human service and non-profit organizations to start small businesses and get self-employed.

In case of those with mental issues or retarded adults, there are many businesses which provide jobs with constant mentoring or counseling. These employers know the problems these employees go through and thus work at creating a balance between supporting employees and demanding they meet their job expectations. The people working here earn self-respect being a productive member of society and no longer feel like a throw away.

The poor especially in developing countries can and should be trained in social entrepreneurship and microcredit. As mentioned earlier, various organizations have been started in South Asia like the Grameen bank in Bangladesh which offers grants and no-collateral loans to poor individuals and groups so that they can start and in most cases, develop their existing small businesses.

The poor may have a running business, but they do not have the means to maximize their profits and earn more money with minimal efforts. It is through these loans that they become members of borrower groups where they are trained at managing loans, have an outlet to share ideas to run small businesses and also offer mutual social support.

These groups also create peer pressure to the members to repay loans wherein the members feel that if they fail or default at repaying the loans, they let down both the group and themselves. It is this strategy of most microcredit and microfinance institutions which has contributed to the success of the strategy wherein poor families slowly come out of poverty and become self-sufficient.

More is discussed about training the members about starting their own micro entrepreneurship in the next chapter.

21. Train them Into Micro Entrepreneurship

It should be known that entrepreneurs in low-income countries are generally micro entrepreneurs operating informally. This is in stark contrast with the successful serial entrepreneurs listed in business magazines. Micro entrepreneurs in poor countries generally start, own and run various businesses at the same time.

They exist in large numbers in the poor parts of the world. They are customers of large and varied range of goods and services and can be distributors for large and small firms where they ensure the distributors' goods and services reach even hard-to-reach markets. Though small, these entrepreneurs give good competition to multinationals as unlike multinationals, they can even arrange to deliver a kilo of onions on a phone call!

Micro entrepreneurs help themselves out of poverty as they learn and know how to effectively use their microcredit loans to eradicate poverty. Such successful micro entrepreneurs can lead to an explosion in growth and popularity, and in the process, transform many economies.

This is why it's important that these poor people need to be trained at micro entrepreneurship to help them learn and use the most effective means of overcoming any impediments they may face.

Obstacles

There are three main obstacles micro entrepreneurs face, which they have to be trained to overcome. Micro entrepreneurs lack basic business skills, don't have access to adequate and necessary information and lack the necessary funds to start their endeavor.

They need to be provided training at entrepreneurship level as their management practices are usually practices they'd seen and used for generations and is nothing near what's taught at leading business schools. Not only illiterate, even literate micro entrepreneurs don't usually have the required basic business skills.

For example, they don't wonder why people buy from them and not others, and if no one bought from them, they didn't ponder whom they buy from. They don't wonder if they are selling their goods to the right customers or if there even better and more attractive other customers and other related business, money and people management questions.

Despite the mobile phone revolution and the success of IT companies in developing countries like India, these micro entrepreneurs don't have access to adequate business information. In other words, they don't know the basic information about buyers, sellers and the large marketplace around them and because of this, they usually end up selling their goods to the wrong people at the wrong time and price.

Many entrepreneurs lack access to cheap, secure and convenient savings, remittance mechanisms and money. Only about 40% people of developing countries actually have access to bank accounts. This is either because bank accounts need minimal balances which is unrealistic for most micro-entrepreneurs of because they need to spend too much time and effort to reach the banks which are usually located far away. This is why they end up paying substantial fees to the 'deposit collectors' who go door to door to collect their savings.

How to overcome them

Though these obstacles may seem daunting to micro entrepreneurship, it is possible to overcome them to produce great micro entrepreneurs. New technologies and business models help unleash the potential of their growth by building the necessary 'soft' infrastructure to drive inclusive growth across the world.

There are now many exciting initiatives in the form of cheap, scalable means of teaching them the necessary skills. For example, the Michael Hay of London Business School offers high-quality business education at low cost globally.

They lead the Business Bridge Initiative which combines online learning with face-to-face tutoring by trained people through a network of local hubs in South Africa and Ghana, and plans to introduce the scheme elsewhere.

Once trained, these micro-entrepreneurs learn to generate improved and more revenue and practices. With training and basic education in concepts like inventory management and quality control, micro entrepreneurs experience better productivity and profitability.

How access to information helps

Regarding access to information, providing the micro entrepreneurs with access to the internet and specially tailored contact through mobiles and wired broadband helps them a lot. For example, farmers benefit through weather, crop related and marketing information sent to their mobile phones through text messages.

They can use this information to decide when to plant and harvest seeds and the best marketing strategies for the product all for their benefit. Besides mobile phones, they should also be trained at using computers to access the internet.

By learning how to use the computer and internet, you can find a splurge in the number of micro-entrepreneurs of internet-based businesses ranging from VoIP telephony to online English lessons to online astrology reading.

Regarding access to money, M-Pesa in Kenya help the economically active people use their mobile phones to transact money despite only a few of them having access to formal bank accounts. Similarly the Nobel Peace Prize winning efforts of Muhammad Yunus and others have helped millions of micro entrepreneurs in many ways like to tide over crises, invest in equipment and build businesses.

Once all these obstacles are overcome, micro entrepreneurs should be trained to know and believe in themselves. They need to realize that they have to be passionate about whatever they are trying to achieve to succeed in their endeavor.

They need to realize that they need to put in lots of hard work, and not expect any results overnight. They should realize that they are assured results with their best efforts and focus on efforts and things they can control.

They have to be trained to realize that the road to success for their venture will be a long one, and that they need to enjoy the journey. Though information and maintaining records are necessary to maintain any business endeavor, they need to realize that they have to at times trust and believe in their gut instinct because sometimes a faint instinct voice is much stronger than logic.

Micro-entrepreneurs need to be trained to be flexible and persistent enough to perform well. While they need to focus on their goals, sometimes some changes and adaptations are necessary for the success of their venture.

Of course, nothing is achieved alone. Micro-entrepreneurs need to know that while it's their dream that made them an entrepreneur, they need their team and employees to reach their goals. No one person is good at everything and all the tasks required to run the show.

This is when it's worth mentioning the importance and reasons of a mentor to a micro-entrepreneur. Whether you like it or not, mentors are a must as I think that sometimes, all it takes is a pat on the back to get a job well done!

22. Assign a Mentor – Sometimes Pat on The Back Does the Job!

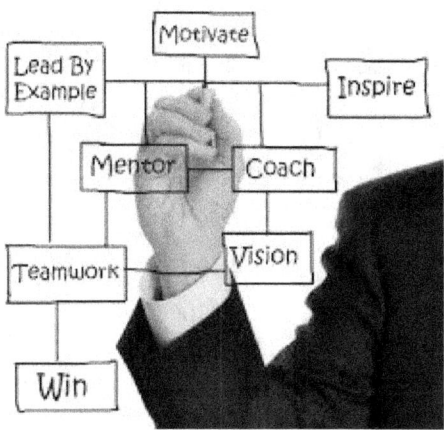

Many successful entrepreneurs state that for every goal they had achieved in life, they have a mentor or a person who had helped them achieve the goal. In fact, though successful, these entrepreneurs proudly say that they did not or could not have accomplished anything alone.

Yes, mentors are necessary not only to the entrepreneurs of developed countries, but also to the many aspiring micro entrepreneurs in developing countries. This is necessary because though personal circumstances, differences in beliefs and orientations and institutional challenges may at times lead to some arguments and difference of opinions between the mentor and the mentored, at the end, it is finally the mentor who gives the mentee a pat on the back for a job well done!

The problem is that the poor do not know or realize the importance of having a mentor. They may in fact consider it a hindrance and obstruction to their realizing their dreams. This is why it's important that they learn and know why they need a mentor. It's only if they really the importance and benefit of having a mentor will they agree to having one.

The importance and necessity of a mentor

Mentors are necessary as they are the ones who will give a kick start onto the path of achievement. No matter what the dream may be, it is a mentor who can give that push or reason to make a move towards the dream.

The dream may at times seem unachievable considering all the hindrances and problems the poverty ridden may face while pursuing their goal. As the mentor has already been in the same position, they know the apprehensions, doubts and hesitations faced at this moment. They can thus provide the spark and guidance for the first step at reaching the micro entrepreneur's goal.

Mentors know exactly what it takes to become a micro entrepreneur and the sacrifices which have to be made. With a mentor knowing exactly where the micro entrepreneur wants to end up, they can provide them with first-hand experience about what they will have to face. This can at times help the entrepreneur decide if they really want and can tread their chosen path.

A mentor's experience can help them see things they hadn't envisioned, and can also help them overcome various obstacles. It is this experience which proves helpful, and this experience is something which cannot be bought anywhere. This experience can only be earned, and is an invaluable tool for anyone to possess to help them reach their goal.

Treading a new path towards a new goal is not an easy one. The micro entrepreneur is entering an entirely new world which they know nothing about. It is only their dreams and aspiration which forms the pushing force for them. They should thus know and be ready to meet lots of uncertainty. It is in situations like this that they require someone to guide them to move ahead.

They will come across many roadblocks on their road to success, and this is where the mentor helps the micro entrepreneur overcome any uncertainties they face, and help them build their confidence levels. though all they give are simple words of encouragement or an email with a different perspective or even do nothing but just stand behind the entrepreneur all the time, it helps a lot in building their mentee's self-confidence.

So all this proves that a mentor is a resource meant for life. In fact, no matter if the micro entrepreneur one day reaches their goals and moves on in life, they will definitely maintain a connection with their mentor. Both mentor and mentee will have such an attachment between each other that they make it a point to periodically meet. They may also call to ask for help and guidance on some things or just to check on each other, even though the mentee may not need a mentor at the time.

Show some appreciation

Of course, it should be remembered that the mentor will do all this expecting something in return. They don't expect any financial benefits, but after taking time from their busy life to help the developing and aspiring micro entrepreneur, they do expect something 'valuable' in return one day. So the mentor may need some help later on, and the mentee should be ready to do it earnestly, no matter how meaningless it may seem to them.

Micro entrepreneurs should not consider it as a chore, but instead, consider it as a means of repayment to their mentor for all their guidance, experiences and professionalism. the mentee can also always show their appreciation to their mentor by writing a hand written thank you note, or remember their mentor and pick up the phone to call them anytime later on in life. The mentee just needs to make sure they show their appreciation for all the efforts and time their mentor had put into helping the entrepreneur reach their goals and vision in life.

Finding/assigning a mentor

Now that the micro entrepreneur realizes the importance and need of having a mentor to help them reach their goals in life, the next question that crops to their mind will naturally be who they should consider as their mentor. Well, while there are some ways and methods entrepreneurs in developed countries can use to find their mentor to help them reach their vision, it's a different picture with the developing countries.

The aspiring micro-entrepreneurs in developing countries don't know any person who will be fit enough to be their mentor. Mentors requires experience and knowledge, which the poor population lacks in.

This is where and why they need to ask whoever suggests the concept to them! This person will in turn have friends or family members who will be ready to help and guide the needy at reaching their goals.

They will in fact vouch for someone, which in turn saves the entrepreneur lots of time and hard work which would have otherwise been spent on tracking someone down. With their mentor in hand, the entrepreneur next has to learn to develop and use a call center approach to implement in their dream project.

23.Develop Call Center Approach –

So now you naturally wonder what exactly is a call center approach? It is a staffing approach developed into a cohesive team which ensures the successful operation of the business. The most important step here involves choosing the right staff to answer their calls.

It is this staffing plan which later affects other decisions based on technology, processes and facilities as they are the people who will be creating a good or bad impression on their customers with the way they answer their calls.

With about three-fourth of the call center costs depending on labor, lots of importance is placed on choosing the right staff. The right people have to be chosen to handle all incoming calls as this will have a great impact on the functioning of the center.

There are various staffing options to choose from:

Outsourcing

Outsourcing in call centers involves contracting some or all of their business functions to a third company to answer some or all of their calls or other types of contracts instead of doing all this in-house. Outsourcing is usually resorted to avoid unnecessary resource drain and expenses related with the setting up and operation of a function which is usually not the business's concentration.

As starting and running a call center is expensive, many companies can save money by outsourcing some tasks. This is a feasible option for start-ups and companies unsure of what their call center needs will be as they can buy call center services as required without investing in any expensive equipment, labor, software or facilities.

Even established companies benefit through outsourcing as they can outsource the handling of calls to experts while they concentrate on other tasks. Besides reduced cost, the other benefit of outsourcing is flexibility. While traditional call centers receive costs in peaks and valleys where their staff and equipment lie idle when there are few calls, the outsourced call centers handle multiple clients' calls to help smooth out both valleys and peaks.

This leads to better use of staff and equipment, where they can handle even spikes in call volume which in-house centers may have difficulty handling because of insufficient telecommunications capacity and staff.

Outsourced call-centers also have well-trained staff which can quickly adapt to different customers' needs. They also have experts on staff who handle various functions on a daily basis to ensure the smooth functioning of answering all types and volumes of calls. Outsourcers also practice effective cost tracking to manage the margin between their costs and the client's price.

Their total monthly cost is shown on the outsourcer's bill each month while in-house operations may have difficult to trace and manage hidden costs to effectively manage the financial aspects of the profitability, running and effectiveness of the business.

Outsourcers use the latest state-of-the-art technology to ensure all customers' calls are professionally handled. With daily performance assessment being part of the agreement with clients, it is more often and thoroughly done than by an in-house center as supervisors may not spend sufficient time and attention to it.

It's not feasible or practical for in-house call centers to perform round the clock seven days a week, 24 hours a day. It can be expensive for them to attend the calls arriving in no peak hours; this is where outsourcers can provide their services at a lower cost and thus help the business maintain 24/7 availability.

In-house staffing

Businesses which prefer handling contacts with their own employees hire and train their own agents to work in their company's call center(s). This involves finding a site, setting up the appropriate call center systems and technology and recruiting and managing their employees.

In-house call centers need to concentrate on getting the right number of people to handle the workload at the right time as three-fourth of call center operating costs depends on staffing. With a systematic schedule of staff requirements and workload, the call center will quickly reach their service goals with efficient operation.

The in-house staff carries out all call center functions like human resources administration, facilities management to maintain an effective workplace based on engineering concepts like lighting, ergonomics, noise and climate and technology management where the right voice and data telecommunications services are provided and implemented in the center. These equipment require a substantial investment along with ongoing maintenance.

The in-house staff also performs quality management by monitoring procedures and technologies to ensure customer satisfaction and also regularly measure and report the staff performance based on a system of metrics.

They also have to create and follow the center's capital and operating budgets by generating profit-and-loss statements. This is especially important if the call center is a revenue-generating one as it is an important part of the center's ongoing operations.

An in-house call center should continuously assess various risks to its operations using contingency plans which includes staffing, telecommunications networks, access channels and call center systems to prevent problems from occurring in a disaster.

Telecommuting

In-house call centers can consider hiring some employees to handle customer contacts and other to work through telecommunication or offsite. Telecommuting has grown rapidly, especially amidst call centers.

With this technology, agents can log in from their home or some other remote site to receive calls just as if they were sitting in the call center. The same data appears on their screens and their statistics are tracked and reported just like in-house agents. Supervisors also monitor and record their calls on a scheduled basis.

Benefits

There are various benefits to using telecommuting in call centers like a flexible schedule. It is difficult and expensive covering peaks and valleys of calls with traditional staff. It's not practical having someone work just two hours in the morning and two hours in the afternoons during peak hours however they can expect someone working from home to do so.

Moreover, night and weekend hours are easier accomplished with telecommuters, and as many people don't like commuting to work at night and in high traffic, telecommuting is a feasible option to them.

Telecommuting helps save in terms of real estate as they need not house the telecommute agent in any physical call center. Not only does the call center save on the rent or lease amount of their call center office, they also save on maintenance costs furniture, conference spaces, lunchrooms, toilets and other amenities.

Telecommuting offers the benefit of hiring from an expanded labor pool which may include highly qualified staff who are physically challenged or handicapped and cannot commute to the business site every day. Homebound caregivers are also another group of potential workers who need to stay at home to look after their babies or elderly patients and can't afford to travel to a workplace but are willing to work from home.

As the telecommuting staff need spend time or money commuting to their office, they are usually willing to work for a lower pay. They oblige to this as they not only save on transportation costs, but also food costs and a work wardrobe.

Telecommuting also helps companies retain their best employees who may have to move to another city or area of the country. Call centers tend to lose various employees because their spouse's job takes them to a near place. Telecommuting helps them remain employed while the center need not recruit and train a new person for the job.

Telecommuting is more productive as they have fewer interruptions distracting them. Moreover, the comfort and increased satisfaction of working from home may lead to an increased productivity.

While disasters and emergencies can disable normal call center functions, telecommuters can help the call center mange its work in these situations. While a flu epidemic, power outages or a flood may prevent staff from reaching the call center, telecommuters can continue working.

Micro entrepreneur needs to choose

It is up to the micro entrepreneur to decide which call center approach they'd prefer working with. It all boils down to their budget, the type of work load they expect and their eventual aim. It is based on the type of call center system they plan to implement that they can hire the required people for the jobs.

They need to hire people who can oversee the entire working of the establishment by creating appropriate work schedules and workloads and by tracking and managing the daily performance, and the employees who will be abiding to the schedule and workload by answering calls on time and all the time.

Micro entrepreneurs should not only know who and how many people to hire, they should also be competent enough to lower or increase staff as per their work requirements. If they notice that there is not much work or productivity going on, its better reducing the workforce or go looking for new clients to ensure their staff have work all the time.

They should make it a point to award their staff with incentives to give their staff more reason to put in their extra efforts to reap these incentives and thus benefit the call center and themselves. All this constitutes workforce management which ensures the call center has the 'right number' of people in staff to respond to their customer needs and minimize costs while meeting service goals. It also include performance management wherein the employees need to be trained to attend as many calls and possible while providing quality service over the phone.

Technology and knowledge management

The next, and large aspect of the call center approach the micro entrepreneur has to implement in their endeavor is effective technology management. As most of the interactions in a call center are over the phone, everything has to be carried out over an efficient telephone network system.

Various peripheral equipment may also be required for an enhanced interaction to automate routine processes and improve performance. For example the automatic call distribution which receives the call, connects it to an agent and even provides queuing and announcements when an agent is unavailable and provides management reports. Its main role is to equally distribute the workload to a group of people and ensure the callers wait the shortest time possible while the workload is fairly distributed to employees.

Desktop tools like computer desktop applications developed to handle the company's product orders, video interactions tools and imaging systems are needed for processing their phone requests and performing the required tasks.

Company specific applications providing customer information files with details of the customer's account, address, phone number, email address, etc. are also required for efficient call center functioning.

The knowledge of the employees have to be efficiently managed for maximum efficiently. Their knowledge has to be captured and made available to people looking for help and information through their phone calls.

Knowledge management systems are thus used to address this need by storing and retrieving data which can be easily searched to find answers. While all these tools do help improve service in complex environments, they require lots of maintenance like data being constantly updated.

The call center approach is no doubt an extensive approach at handling any business venture. However it is an effective approach which ensures maximum productivity and efficiency at reaching any goal. In addition to this, the use of online counseling and MIS systems will help the micro entrepreneur run their business.

24. Online Counselling and MIS systems

THE SOLUTION: MANAGEMENT INFORMATION SYSTEMS

* Management Information Systems (MIS) — A business function, like accounting and human resources, which moves information about people, products, and processes across the company to facilitate decision-making and problem-solving

With the micro entrepreneur venturing into a new venture, they may come across various obstacles. While their mentor is around to help them overcome this, at times, the mentor may have their own commitments or may not have sufficient knowledge or experience about the relevant doubt or problem. This is when it is better to approach an online counsellor for some online counselling.

Online counsellors to entrepreneurs are professionals at the job who know all the psychological, social and economic factors related to selecting, preparing and running an entrepreneurial career. They are thus capable and adept at discussing various doubts and apprehensions with aspiring entrepreneurs so that they achieve their goals.

Moreover, with psychological stress being part and parcel of any creative and entrepreneurial activity, entrepreneurs may go through stress at various stages in the development of their enterprise. This is when they benefit from professional online counselling who will be able to help them relax and overcome the stress by providing them with possible solutions to the problems.

The entrepreneur is embarking on a new venture, in a new land and space in their lives. They naturally come across various situations they had never expected, and need help overcoming and facing the situation. The counselors thus help entrepreneurs develop context-specific tacit knowledge about their ventures. This influences the new venture's performance by increasing the odds of its start-up.

MIS systems

In addition to online counselling, micro entrepreneurs need and get lots of help through MIS systems. MIS is the acronym for Management Information Systems which are systems used for collecting and processing raw data into useful information which is then disseminated to the user in their required format. It contains information which helps managements feel the organization's pulse and helps them take decisions accordingly.

If the right and good business practices are followed, these MIS can offer various benefits to the business, like sustainability, increased efficiency and productivity, better decision making, greater urban and rural outreach and faster delivery of products and services.

MISs have various uses like providing a consolidated view of linked data of customers and groups. MIS reduces the chances of any duplication of effort while increasing the speed of work, supports workflow and procedures for users and can be easily ported to even remote areas using laptop or palm technology.

Provides a complete functional and integration solution

A good MIS solution provides a complete functional and integration solution for the business. It can handle large volumes of data to handle the growing needs of any organization. In fact, it should grow with the organization, which is important as some organizations may grow rather quickly.

Good MIS solutions are flexible. They are parameter driven where the user can put in their business rules for the MIS, which accepts new products and customers. The MIS should also be able to handle various institution types and get implemented in various organizations, and not be limited to a single institutional model.

Successful MIS solutions are those which is easily deployed and adapted by the end user. It should have a familiar and friendly user interface and preferably window based, the most popular OS today.

The screen display should be logical and consistent with language, format and functions while data entry should be easy for the user to understand. The MIS should also be capable of generating various predefined reports and user defined reports created as per the needs and requirements of the organization.

As the database is the heart of an organization, the MIS solution should be able to restrict access to it through login id, etc., have built in safeguards and be adequately protected against virus attacks. It should have a regular backup feature so that the user is protected against sabotage or system failure and be easily and accurately restarted from the stored data.

The system should be able to continue functioning and notify the user whenever problems like unreliable power supply occurs, and be able to accurately restart when the problem is resolved. The system should have support infrastructure and maintenance service available to provide timely maintenance to ensure the system runs effectively all the time. Like any software, the MIS should also be upgraded with new functionalities added to it as the organization grows.

So with the right MIS system integrated into the organization, the micro entrepreneur is assured that their enterprise is effectively administered with minimal hassles. The MIS solution takes care of most of the organization and management work of the institution.

Of course, this is possible only if the correct and accurate data is fed to the MIS solution, and if the micro entrepreneur is first trained into the right use of the system. If the entrepreneur does not know how to use the system, it may end up doing more harm than good to the venture!

Now comes the three M's which are crucial for the success of any venture; Monitor, Mentor and Motivation. Anyone pursuing a new venture needs someone around to always monitor what is being done, be a mentor and also give the necessary motivation where required. Those in the developing country may not understand or realize the importance of all this unless its' importance is clearly defined and described.

Why motivate

Monitoring is important at the global level to identify and document successful programs and approaches, and to track the progress towards common indictors of related projects. At the program level, monitoring helps systematically track implementations and outputs to measure the effectiveness of the program.

Constant monitoring helps decide if the program is on track and if any changes are needed. In other words, monitoring is the basis for modification of interventions and assesses the quality of activities the micro-entrepreneur conducts.

Monitoring also helps decide if the program has reached its expected outcomes, and if it has been effectively implemented. This information is important in making informed decisions about the working of programs and develop objective conclusions about the success of a program.

What can be learned in general while monitoring micro-entrepreneurs?

What strategies are most effective at generating maximum productivity and responsiveness from the work force?

What can give the employees the necessary push to excel at their skills?

What are the most common obstacles faced by micro entrepreneurs?

What are the social, economic, political, cultural and other hurdles micro entrepreneurs face?

What investments give the most promising results and how much do they cost?

Are the specific activities being carried out as planned? Why and why not?

Are there any amendments to be made?

Mentors

Mentoring is important in any establishment, no matter if it's at an amateur or professional level. Micro entrepreneurs in poor and developing countries especially need mentors as they are venturing into a new niche, pursuing their dreams. Mentors help in many ways, and are indeed necessary for the success of any venture.

Mentors offer the benefit of their perspective and experience in their field. They can assimilate to a new position and give an insider's view on how to do things. They helps a lot in the progress of the venture, and even helps people advance in their career.

Mentors have the capacity of thinking out of the box, and thus help the micro entrepreneur look at situations in different ways. They ask difficult questions which the micro entrepreneur has to solve. This gives the entrepreneur a 'growth spurt' both at work and personally and helps them overcome all their challenges.

Mentors help at both defining, and reaching long term goals by ensuring the entrepreneur does not lose focus even with everyday distractions. Under the guidance of a mentor, the mentor learns how to develop and bring out the best in themselves.

Whenever the micro entrepreneur has to meet their mentor, they make sure they have completed all the tasks discussed in the last meeting. Thus the mentor develops responsibility and accountability in the mentee. Moreover the excitement of completing tasks and seeing results motivates them to hold themselves accountable for their actions, and makes them reach heights they previously thought were impossible.

One person the entrepreneur can trust with their ideas and vision is their mentor. No matter if they have a technical problem, a problem with the staff, an ethical problem or just need some help and advice on tackling new hurdles, they can trust and confide in their mentor. Consequently, as the mentor will be sharing some of their personal stories and experiences, it's important that the mentee also respects this confidentiality and does not disclose the secrets to others.

Mentors make great friends who the mentee can share all their life's ups and downs with. Mentors mentor the mentee only because they know that the mentee has the capacity to do something in life, and just need the right guidance and push to reach their goals. It is with this ideal that they support their mentee and bring out the best in them.

Similarly, the mentee should also prove that themselves worthy and build trust with the mentor. Mentees should also share their experiences, views and just open up as the mentor can help only if they thoroughly understand the mentee.

Mentors are especially important and necessary to a micro entrepreneur as they can help expand the mentee's network of contacts and business acquaintances. As the entrepreneur is entering a new world, they obviously will not know many people in their field.

They need to get to know as many people as possible and broaden their network, which is all possible through their mentor. Similarly, mentors have the power and ability of opening doors in companies and boards to help their mentee.

The micro entrepreneur can and will work better while under the wings of their mentor. The mentor paints a clear picture of the future, and what has to be done next to help the mentee know in which direction they need to move. This in turn helps the entrepreneur feel more confident about their idea and project which in turn leads to better job performance and venture success.

Motivation

Last, but not least, the entrepreneur needs some motivation to get the push to move ahead towards their dream and goal. In fact, no venture or business moves ahead or flourishes without any goal setting and the necessary motivation! Motivation in fact adds spark to life and the venture and makes starting the venture look so much easier!

Goals are very important in any venture as it turns aspirations into tangible objects which require both commitment and action. In case of a micro entrepreneur, their goals include the specific guidelines set for the project, the necessary details and also the necessary resources they seek to reach their vision.

With their set goals, the business and employees get a means of gauging the direction they want their business to go. These goals are usually, and preferably set with credence to established business models, overall objectives and mission statements.

Micro entrepreneurs also benefit from motivation as it has an impact on both mental and physical human reactions. Once motivated, employees carry out their tasks with added zeal which in turn leads to higher productivity and revenue with reduced cost but satisfied owners.

Without any motivation, the employees end up working slower without much regard or emphasis to productivity or efficiency and this eventually costs the business money. Most of the time a lack of motivation is due to the absence of direction or purpose, which can be revered just by introducing goals.

These goals should be well-defined goals which are well defined and within the grasp of reality. This means it has to adhere to the micro entrepreneur's company's primary objectives and scope of work to provide positive and real motivation. It's possible to raise motivation to productive levels only if the company has a positive attitude, working atmosphere and working culture.

Moreover, all businesses should understand that a positive environment is very necessary as if the workplace surroundings is full of negativity, it only creates stress and pressure on employees who in turn lose the motivation and dreams of reaching their goals.

Besides goals and motivation, entrepreneurs should use the help of incentives to the goal to generate a positive impact on their employees. Motivation improves if and when employees see a reward in their way which in turn gives a better chance at reaching their mission goals.

Last but not least, motivation brings about change, just like the flickering flames. The micro entrepreneur may start out the venture with one reason or idea which may change as they progress. It is the motivation to reach these changing goals and ideas which fuels the entrepreneur to move forward.

And it is this motivation which gives a sense of satisfaction even if the entrepreneur doesn't accomplish what they had set out to do as it ensures there never is a loss of hope or believe in visions and ideals of life.

It is thus a combination and the right proportions of monitoring, mentoring and motivation which helps the micro entrepreneur stay focused and stick to their dreams. Entrepreneurs are enterprising people, and don't usually stick to one project.

Once entrepreneurs from developing countries learn how easy and possible it is for them to reach their dreams and they get successful with their venture, they progress towards eradicating poverty in their country. Their venture not only helps improve their country's economy, they also provide employment to so many other poor people.

The widespread benefits of one venture helps the micro entrepreneur realize the importance of their ventures in eradicating poverty. This in turn provides them with inspiration for new ideas to implement and goals to reach. In the process they may require new employees and staff and repeat the entire startup process again.

Instead of looking for new staff, it's better if they rope in their alumni. Not only will they help them increase their outreach, they also have entrepreneurship experience and prove to be a worthy asset to the new venture. Read on to learn more about this.

26.Bring them back as Alumni and increase your Out reach

OUTREACH & ALUMNI RELAT

Yes, it's a fact. Former employees are not considered by as assets and not turncoats in both developed and developing countries. They are given the same attention vested out to alumni of universities by keeping in touch with departed workers so that they can return to their 'alumni' or employer to work as brand ambassadors, recruiters and salespeople.

This concept is a relatively new one conceptualized by McKinsey, a management consultant where a promotion system leaves a steady stream of staff who leaves the firm on relatively friendly terms. These ex-employees usually move on to work for potential clients and not rival consulting firms.

And in this case, they can also be brought back to help with the company or micro entrepreneur if required. This alumni benefits the new venture and micro entrepreneur in many ways. While the most obvious benefit is that they can and will buy new products or services rendered by the micro entrepreneur, they also offer the following benefits:

Cheaper to hire

It is actually cheaper hiring an ex-employee than a brand new person. This is because the rehires are generally 40% more productive in their first quarter at work and tend to stay longer at the job. Moreover, as they are known quantities, the risk of an expensive misfire is completely eliminated. The alumni also have a growing list of referrals where some companies are even more than ready to offer alumni compensation for all hired referrals!

Great source of ideas

Employee alumni have lots of ideas and knowledge which can help the micro entrepreneur with their existing and new venture. Old employees can also help companies understand what competitors are doing, and what people are doing to eradicate poverty throughout the world. Alumni can be hired either during periods of high demand when there's lots of work to be done, or just use their expertise.

Effective marketers and ambassadors

Past employees play a huge influence on creating an opinion of the organization, especially if they haven't been gone from the organization for long. Maintaining good relations with them can thus help improve the company's reputation, brand and influence. They can give the organization a much-needed outside perspective as they will be able and ready to point out uncomfortable truths. An alum can give a better and more honest feedback for a new product than a current employee.

Investors

Employees leaving a company generally hold some shares of its stocks as part of their investment or retirement plans. By maintaining good relations with these employees, there is an increased chance of their holding onto the shares for a longer time or may even buy more shares.

How to bring them back

It may seem complicating launching an alumni program as the company has to gather and manage large amounts of information. However the internet and data-processing technologies help launch programs on the following basis:

Better exit process

Relationships with the alumni are best seeded when the employee leaves the organization. The HR or rather micro entrepreneur could explain the benefits of maintaining relations and staying in touch, collect their contact information and ask them their reasons for leaving and their views of the company.

Two-way contact

The micro entrepreneur has to offer their employees some reason or benefit to maintain relations with the alumni. Some benefits worth offering the alumni are semi-proprietary intellectual capital, invitations to events and social gatherings and free or subsidized training programs.

Help hiring great people

The micro entrepreneur can depend on the alumni to help recruit great candidates for the business. They not only help source the candidates, but also help with reference checks and judging cultural fits. They know who the best candidates for the job are as they know what skills and knowledge are essential for the particular job role.

So in a nutshell, a corporate alumni network can indeed help strengthen the micro entrepreneur's brand. They are a cheaper employment option which can effectively help increase the brand's outreach. The increased outreach helps generate more employment opportunities to the needy and in the process, helps a lot at eradicating poverty.

27.Compliments - Sleep well! Good wishes

Now that was a mouthful, wasn't it? It all boils down to helping the poor come out of poverty so that they can live a decent life with decent meals like you and me. We can help them come out of their misery just by giving them a push here and there.

Through this book you now know about so many organizations, ventures and people out there who have started out on this mission of eradicating poverty. We have facilities like:

- the Grameen Bank and M-Pesa,
- mobile banking
- micro financing
- mentoring
- mind mapping
- social entrepreneurship
- technology
- call center approach
- training of the necessary skills
- how the alumni can help and much more

which if implemented correctly, can indeed help eradicate poverty in this world and make the world a much better place to live in in a few years' time. Instead of just pondering on the problem, it's now time for us to do something for the less fortunate.

Once you accomplish this feat, you are sure to feel a sense of accomplishment which will give you a good night's sleep knowing you have done well for someone. Knowing that someone out there who once did not have a roof over their head now do and can finally have a good night's sleep.

www.ingramcontent.com/pod-product-compliance
Lightning Source LLC
Chambersburg PA
CBHW071344280526

45787CB00001B/219